MW00471182

How to Be Free
from Bitterness

How to Be Free from Bitterness

JIM WILSON

COMMUNITY CHRISTIAN MINISTRIES
MOSCOW, IDAHO

Published by
Community Christian Ministries | ccmbooks.org
P. O. Box 9754, Moscow ID 83843 | 208.883.0997

Jim Wilson, *How to Be Free from Bitterness*, Copyright © 1995, 1999, 2003, 2004, 2017, 2019 by James I. Wilson
Study Questions and Next Steps in *How to Be Free from Bitterness* Copyright © 2003, 2004, 2017, 2019 by Marjorie Dykema
First Edition 1995. Second CCM Edition 2007.

Cover illustration by Forrest Dickison. Interior layout by Valerie Anne Bost. Author photo by Mark LaMoreaux, lamoreauxphoto.com.

Scripture quotations are from the the Holy Bible, New International Version®, NIV® Copyright © 1973, 1978, 1984, 2011 by Biblica, Inc.® Used by permission. All rights reserved worldwide.

All rights reserved. No part of this publication may be reproduced, stored in a retrieval system, or transmitted in any form by any means, electronic, mechanical, photocopy, recording, or otherwise, without prior permission of the author, except as provided by USA copyright law.

20 21 22 23 24 25 26 27 28 29   9 8 7 6 5 4 3 2 1

Contents

Preface

*T*he first part of this book on getting rid of bitterness and forgiving others has been presented many times over the last forty years at many retreats and Bible conferences. Thousands of the taped messages and audio downloads have been distributed in the U.S. and abroad. Chris LaMoreaux transcribed one of those tapes, and, after much editing, we printed 1,000 copies of it as a book. Since that time, more than 300,000 copies of *How to Be Free from Bitterness* have been sold or given away.

Heather Wilson Torosyan is my daughter, the wife of Ararat Torosyan and mother of Yeran, Masis, and Sevan. She was a Christian worker in Egypt for eight months and in Turkey for about five years. Chris Vlachos ran His Place, our bookstore in Provo, Utah. His primary ministry is teaching at Salt Lake Seminary.

We would like to thank Marjorie Dykema for her work in developing study guide questions for each article.

If you wish to order more copies, you can do so at www.ccmbooks.org/bookstore or by contacting CCM:

Community Christian Ministries
P. O. Box 9754, Moscow ID 83843-0180
Phone/Fax: 208.883.0997 | E-mail: ccm@moscow.com

This publication has been translated into the following languages: Afrikaans, Armenian, Albanian, Chinese-simplified, Chinese-traditional, Dutch, French, Japanese, Korean, Polish, Portuguese, Russian, Scots Gaelic, Spanish, Swahili, Tagalog, Telegu, and Urdu.

If you would like to translate this publication into another language, please contact Community Christian Ministries.

JIM WILSON
Moscow, Idaho

How to Be Free From Bitterness

Jim Wilson

Get rid of all bitterness, rage and anger, brawling and slander, along with every form of malice. Be kind and compassionate to one another, forgiving each other, just as in Christ God forgave you. Be imitators of God, therefore, as dearly loved children, and live a life of love, just as Christ loved us and gave himself up for us as a fragrant offering and sacrifice to God. (Eph. 4:31–5:2)

---

*I*n our text, we are instructed to get rid of all bitterness. Before we begin discussing how and why this must be done, it is crucial to realize that the basis for all our actions in this regard must be what Jesus Christ has done for us on the cross. In all our actions, we are to be imitators of God.

In the Old Testament, there was a woman whose name meant Pleasant. Her name was Naomi, and she had moved from Israel to another land with her husband and sons. But her husband had died, and within the next ten years both of her sons died.

She made some comments to her recently widowed daughters-in-law about it. Ruth 1:13b: "It is more bitter for me than for you, because the LORD's hand has gone out against me!" She was comparing in order to determine who had the right to be more bitter.

In Ruth 1:20–21: "Don't call me Naomi," she told them. "Call me Mara, because the Almighty has made my life very bitter. I went away full, but the LORD has brought me back empty. Why call me Naomi? The LORD has afflicted me; the Almighty has brought misfortune upon me."

Her bitterness was toward God. It was God who had taken away her husband; it was God who had taken away her sons, and she held it against Him. Five times in these three verses she held God accountable for her bitterness.

There are many people like this today. Not only are they bitter; they enjoy being bitter. They somehow like it, and they feed on it. They wouldn't know what to do if they got rid of it; they wouldn't have a purpose for living. They like being bitter.

We know people like that in the world, and we know people like that in the church. It is easy to recognize when someone is bitter. You can see it in the eyes and in the lines of the face—even if the person is young. You can see it in their mouth; you can see it when they're smiling or laughing. You can hear it in the tone of their voice. You can hear it when they protest that they are not bitter. The bitterness is central, and it pervades everything.

There are bitter people in the Bible besides Naomi. In fact, there are quite a few. For example, Jonah was a bitter man. The Lord said to him, "Do you have a right to be angry about the vine?"

"I do," he said. "I am angry enough to die" (Jonah 4:9). He thought he had a right to his anger. I like being angry. God, you are wrong to forgive people. I don't want you to forgive people.

People enjoy holding things against other people. But our text requires us to remove all bitterness and to maintain a tender heart.

Here's the question: Is it possible to be kind, compassionate, tenderhearted, and yet bitter at the same time? These are all interior attitudes. Tenderheartedness, by definition, involves a tender heart. Bitterness is also on the inside. But it is not possible to have two different, contradictory attitudes on the inside.

Paul says to get rid of all bitterness, and to be kind and compassionate one to another. Therefore, the bitterness must go. But before it can be removed, it is necessary to know what it is—and that it is there.

It is relatively easy to see when other people are bitter. But it's not so easy to see it in ourselves. It is therefore important to have a good understanding of the Bible's definition of the problem.

Let us suppose that a Christian commits a sin. He tells a lie, for instance. When he tells this lie, does he feel guilty, or does he feel bitter? The answer is guilty. When we sin, we feel guilty. It is straightforward. Now suppose that someone told a lie about this same Christian and spread it all over town. What does he feel now—guilt or bitterness?

Guilt is what we feel when we sin, and bitterness is what we feel when others sin against us. The very definition of bitterness points to the action of another. If we had committed the offense, we would feel guilty and would know that we had to confess and forsake our sin. We might not confess the sin when we are guilty, but not because we did not know what to do. But what do we do with the guilt of others?

Bitterness is always based upon someone else's sin—whether real or imagined. Consider the imaginary sin first. Many times we can be bitter toward someone for what he said, when in reality he did not say it. We heard a false report, and now we are bitter. We wait for an apology which he cannot offer. Shall we remain in bitterness the rest of our lives because he never says he is sorry for something he did not do?

Incidentally, many bitter people cannot imagine the possibility that they are bitter over imaginary sins. As far as bitterness is concerned, the other person's guilt is always real. For such a person trying to be free from bitterness, it is acceptable for them to assume that the guilt of the other person is real, so long as they get rid of their own bitterness.

But what about genuine sin? There are many bitter people who really were mistreated by the offender. So how do we deal with a genuine offense?

Bitterness is based on sin that somehow relates to you. It is not concerned with how big the sin is; it is based upon how close it is. For instance, if some great and gross immorality occurs in Iran, Iraq, El Salvador, or Colombia, what do we do? We read about it, but we will not feel guilty. We read about it, but we will not feel bitter. We might be appalled or amazed, but we do not feel guilty, and we do not feel bitter, even though it was an awful sin, and someone actually committed it. So it does not depend on how great the evil is; it depends on how close the other person is to me. Bitterness is related to those people who are close.

Who are likely candidates? The answer is simple: fathers, mothers, brothers, sisters, husbands, wives, children, boyfriends, girlfriends, roommates, immediate superiors, immediate subordinates, co-workers, business partners, and maybe some other relatives—grandparents, uncles, etc. There are even many people who are bitter against God.

We do not get bitter towards evil outside of our own immediate contact. Bitterness is based upon the sin of someone who is close to us and who did something to us. It might be minor. It does not have to be great; it just has to be close. Does he pick up his socks? No? Can you get bitter over that? Well, no, but what if he does it 5,000 times?

You may think you have a right to be bitter. But the Bible does not grant anyone the right to be bitter. The text says to get rid of all bitterness.

"See to it that no one misses the grace of God and that no bitter root grows up to cause trouble and defile many" (Heb. 12:15). Here it describes bitterness as if it were a root. A root is something that is underground and cannot be seen. But there can be visible evidence of its presence, as when sidewalks are lifted.

The fact that you cannot see roots does not mean they are not there. Neither does it mean you will never see them. They drink in nourishment, and they do not stay roots. Eventually they come up.

The fruit that is born bears a direct relation to the root that is producing it. The roots of an apple tree provide us with apples. If there is a bitter root, it will bear bitter fruit.

That is what this verse is saying. Beware lest any root of bitterness spring up, cause trouble, and defile many people, which means to make many people filthy. Have you ever seen bitterness go through a church? Bitterness can go through a congregation like a prairie fire. It can go through the work place or a dormitory. Why is this? Somebody decided to share. He was bitter, and he let the root come to the surface and bear fruit. He shared it, and many people became bitter. The author of Hebrews warns us about this. He says beware of missing the grace of God. When you allow it, bitterness comes up and defiles many people. It makes many people filthy.

What happens to a person if he keeps bitterness on the inside for many years? What happens to him physically? Suppose it is bitterness toward some member of the family. He has not shared it. He has not defiled many people—he has kept it down inside. When he keeps it in for some years, he finally begins to hurt. He goes to the doctor, and the doctor says, "You are right; you are sick. But your sickness is not the kind I deal with. I am going to send you to the other kind of doctor."

So he sends him to the psychiatrist, and the psychiatrist agrees. "Yes, you are sick all right. And I know why. You are sick because of 20 years of bitterness towards your father. You have kept it suppressed all these years, and it's rotted out your insides. You have kept this poison within, and this acid on the inside has made you just physically ill. So what I want you to do is to go home and share it with your father. Why keep it in and get sick? Let it out. Get everybody else sick."

So the world has two solutions. Keep the bitterness in and make yourself sick, or let it out and spread the sickness around. God's solution is to dig up the root. Get rid of it. But this takes the grace of God. A man must know the Lord Jesus Christ to be able to do this. He is the source of grace.

Christians should not use the world's solutions for bitterness. When Christians copy the world, they have two poor choices. The Bible says to get rid of all bitterness. You must not keep it in, and you must not share it. Surrender it to the Father, through the Son.

"But if you harbor bitter envy and selfish ambition in your hearts, do not boast about it or deny the truth. Such 'wisdom' does not come down from heaven but is earthly, unspiritual, of the devil. For where you have envy and selfish ambition, there you find disorder and every evil practice" (James 3:14–15).

When I was a young midshipman at the Naval Academy, I thought that the pettiness and jealousy I observed would give way to maturity. I thought the higher you got in rank, the more mature you became, the less this sort of thing occurred. But as I grew older, I found out that the jealousy just got more intense. Bitterness accumulates. Unless there's a solution to it, people do not get less bitter with maturity. They get more bitter over the years. It gets worse and worse.

And if you harbor bitter envy, evil practice will result. It does not come from heaven. It is straight from the pit and is of the devil. Every evil practice results from this attitude. As should be obvious, we have a real problem. How do we get rid of bitterness?

Before we can get rid of bitterness, we have to realize that we are bitter. How can we tell if we are bitter? One good rule of thumb is this: Bitterness remembers details. You have had thousands of conversations in your life, most of which you have forgotten. But this one took place five years ago, and you remember every single word, his intonation, and every inflection of his voice. You know exactly what happened—which means you are bitter.

Someone might object and say that it is also possible to have a good memory of a wonderful conversation. Is this possible? Yes, but not likely. Why? Because memory is helped by review, review, and more review. People do not usually mull over the wonderful things as much. But they do go over and over and over the bad things. I have done quite a bit of counseling with people who are in the process of getting divorced. I have known some of them since they were married, at a happier time in their life. But at the time of the divorce, they cannot remember a single happy time. All they can remember is what they have gone over and over. They are bitter.

This doesn't mean there were not happy times. It just means that they have concentrated on how right they were and how wrong the other person was. If someone has a sharp, detailed memory for things which happened years ago when he was a child or a young man or woman, and that memory is at all accusative of anyone, then it is an indication of bitterness. And the solution for bitterness is to get rid of it.

I had a wonderful experience one time in Dallas, Texas. I was speaking on a Saturday night at the home of an old friend. Because I was going to be in Dallas, I wrote notes to several people that I knew in the area, and they showed up at this home.

My host asked me to speak on bitterness, which I did. Afterwards, a couple came up to see me. I had known them eight years before in Pullman, Washington. The wife said, "We have been married for eight years. The first year of marriage, I was so bitter toward my mother that I laid it on my husband every single day. Our first year of marriage was just awful because I kept sharing this bitterness toward my mother with my husband."

Then she told me that seven years earlier I had spoken on bitterness, and she had gotten rid of hers. One day, she saw another woman who was really bitter towards her mother. She thought, "I can help that woman. I can share all the common experiences. I went to her to share this, and I couldn't remember any of the details. My detailed memory had gone. All I could tell her was I used to remember things, and I do not remember them anymore." The Lord had really taken care of her bitterness.

Another time, I was teaching a four-week course on marriage. I had put a notice in the paper and did not know who would show up. A woman came who had been referred to the class by a doctor. I can honestly say that I have never seen anyone more bitter in appearance in my life. She had forty years of accumulated bitterness. She got rid of it that night and made an appointment to see me the next day at the bookstore where I worked. She came into the store, and I did not know who she was. She looked so different. I had just met her the night before, but she was clean inside now.

What is the problem? Why do we not get rid of bitterness? If I tell a lie, I can confess it and be forgiven. In order to get rid of it, I have to bring it back to my own heart. We need to bring the realization of bitterness back to our own hearts. Instead, the temptation is to look at the offender. Look what he did. That is the nature of bitterness. In order to get rid of it, I need to recognize that it is my problem before I can confess and forsake it.

You say, "I am not bitter. I just get hurt easily." But the symptoms of getting hurt are very close to the symptoms of resentment. Do you know what instant resentment is? You might say. "It is not bitterness—it is just hurt feelings." But there is a close relationship between being hurt and being resentful. Someone gets hurt, and he gets resentful. There is another very close connection between resentment and bitterness. Resentment turns into a deep bitterness.

Bitterness is just resentment that has been held on to. It has become rancid and rotten. It is kept in, and it gets worse.

The links in the chain continue. There is a connection between bitterness and hatred, and a very clear biblical identification between hatred and murder. What I am saying is that hurt can lead to murder. Some might object that this teaching is too strong. But the strength of it is from the Bible.

What we want to do is make it apparent how sinful bitterness is. The bitter person must first recognize that he is bitter, and secondly, that it is a gross evil. Again, the reason people do not deal with this sin is that they think it is the other person's sin. The devil says, "Well, when he quits lying, or he quits doing this or that, or when he says he's sorry, then you will feel better."

But suppose he does not quit? Suppose he never quits? Are you going to be bitter for the rest of your life because someone else insists on being in sin? That does not make any sense at all. You may say, "I will forgive him when he says he is sorry, but not until then. I have a right to my bitterness until then. When he says he is sorry, I will forgive him and everything will be fine." You keep this wall of bitterness up, and one day he comes to you and he says, "I'm sorry." Can you forgive him now? No, because bitterness doesn't forgive. In order to forgive this person when he says he is sorry, you have to be ready before he says he is sorry. And if you are ready to forgive him before he says he is sorry, then it doesn't depend on whether he says he is sorry or not. In other words, you get rid of bitterness unilaterally. It does not matter what the other person does.

Earlier I made the point that bitterness seems to stem from the other person's sin—real or imagined. That is only how it appears. In reality, bitterness is a sin that stands alone. The bitter person decides to be bitter independently of the offender.

You say, "No, he sinned against me, and when he says he is sorry everything will be fine." That is not true. I have known situations where an apology was offered, and the person is still bitter. Suppose the offender is dead and cannot apologize. I know people who are extremely bitter, and the bitterness is towards their parents who died years ago. But the bitterness has not died. Bitterness is the sin of the bitter person alone, unrelated to anyone else.

One time around Christmas, I went to the Walla Walla State Penitentiary to spend the day with the inmates. I spent about six hours there. During the afternoon, I was in maximum security, talking about and teaching evangelism. One fellow asked about reaching the really hard-core criminals. I thought he was really interested in such evangelism and talked to him about it. Then I spent time in minimum security, protective custody, and other places. In the evening, I was back in maximum security, and thought I would talk on the subject of bitterness. I figured there were probably some bitter people there.

The same fellow who had asked about evangelism in the afternoon asked me another question. He said, "How can you get rid of bitterness towards somebody who beat up your three-year-old son unmercifully?"

I told him how, and then I said, "You know, when you get rid of your bitterness you can help this person so that he won't beat up other little kids."

He said, "No, this guy cannot be helped."

I said, "Sure, he can."

"No, no."

"Why not?"

"He is not with us anymore."

This inmate had murdered him. He had murdered him because of what he had done to his three-year-old son—that's why he was in prison. But even though he had killed the man, he was still bitter. In other words, expressing his bitterness did not get rid of it. Nor did the death get rid of it.

When someone else says he is sorry, it does not get rid of our bitterness. The only thing that gets rid of it is confession before God because of the Lord Jesus Christ's death and resurrection. This is the only solution.

You may say that the person you are bitter toward died many years ago. You did not kill the person like the man in prison. Otherwise, there is no difference; the other person is dead, and you are still bitter.

If the person who died was a believer, he is with the Lord, forgiven and pure. You are bitter towards someone who is rejoicing in Heaven because his name is written in the Lamb's book of life.

If the person who died was not a believer, then he is under the judgement of God described in 2 Thessalonians 1:6–8: "God is just: He will pay back trouble to those who trouble you and give relief to you who are troubled, and to us as well. This will happen when the Lord Jesus is revealed from heaven in blazing fire with his powerful angels. He will punish those who do not know God and do not obey the gospel of our Lord Jesus."

"Do not take revenge, my friends, but leave room for God's wrath, for it is written: 'It is mine to avenge; I will repay,' says the Lord" (Rom. 12:19). God is just, and God does the paying.

Even if these people were alive, they could not take care of your bitterness, nor could you by going after them. Being dead, they have been taken care of, either way. That leaves you, alive and bitter, hurting yourself and everyone around you for years. Your bitterness is your sin, regardless of what you think caused it. God will allow you to experience the forgiveness and joy that is yours when you repent and confess your bitterness as a great sin against God. We must not keep it, and we must not share it with others. There is only one thing to do, and that is to confess it as a great and evil sin. We must be as persistent in the confession as necessary.

Once I was speaking in Monterey, California, at the U.S. Naval Postgraduate School. There was a man there who had a great reputation as a Bible teacher. He was a line officer in the Navy, but he had been passed over for the command of a submarine, and he was bitter. I spoke on confession of sin and bitterness, and he was really wiped out. He came and saw me and got rid of his bitterness. The next morning, his wife said to me, "I've got a new husband." He had been bitter toward the Navy, but it was his sin, not the Navy's.

Amy Carmichael has a note in her little book *If*: "For a cup brimful of sweet water cannot spill even one drop of bitter water, however suddenly jolted."[1]

1 Amy Carmichael, *If* (Fort Washington, PA: Christian Literature Crusade, n.d.) p. 46.

If a cup is full of sweet water and is jolted, what will come out of it? Sweet water. If you give it a harder jolt, what's going to spill? More sweet water. If someone is filled with sweet water and someone else gives him a jolt, what will come out? Sweet water. Jolts do not turn sweet water into bitter water. That is done by something else.

Jolts only bring out of the container what is already in it. If you are filled with sweetness and light and you get jolted, you're going to spill sweetness and light. If you're filled with honey, the honey will come out. If vinegar comes out, what does that prove? It shows what was already in the container. In other words, much bitterness is not based upon what the other person did at all. It is the result of what we do and are.

Many years ago, I was working in our bedroom at my desk. My wife Bessie was reading in bed. Whatever I was doing wasn't going well. Bessie said something to me, and I turned around and let her have it. It was something un-Christian. She looked at me in amazement and got up and left the room. I sat there thinking, "She should not have said it. Look what she said. Look, look, look." I did that for around 10 minutes. I was bitter towards Bessie, but all she did was jolt the cup. What was in the cup came out.

If I had been filled with sweetness and light, the jolt would not have mattered. I sat there and thought about what she did. I knew better, because I had already learned this truth about bitterness. Still, I thought about her "sin" because there is enjoyment in accusing the other person. Some people do this for years.

I sat there for a while and then got up and went over to my side of the bed, got on my knees, and said, "Lord, I was the only one at fault. It was my bitterness and my sin. I am confessing it, forsaking it, and please forgive me."

I got up off my knees and said, "But look what she said." I got back on my knees.

"God, I'm sorry for what I did. I accept the responsibility. It was my sin, and mine only."

I got up off my knees and said, "God, you and I know who is really at fault." I knelt back down. I stayed on my knees for 45 minutes until I could get up and not say, "Look what she said."

I do not remember now what Bessie said, and I do not remember what I was doing at the desk. I do not remember the details. The only thing I remember now is getting up. But I also know that if I had not taken care of the bitterness I would know to this day exactly what she had said. That is the nature of bitterness.

In order to get rid of bitterness, I have to see that it is evil, and that it is my sin and my sin only. I do not get rid of it through the other person saying he is sorry. I do not get rid of it if the other person quits or dies. I do not get rid of it any other way except calling it sin against the holy God, confessing it, and receiving forgiveness.

The difficulty is getting my eyes off the other person's sin. But just the fact that I think it is his problem shows that it is not. If it actually were his problem, and I were filled with sweetness and light, and not bitter, then I would be concerned about him. I could say, "That poor guy! Look what he did. If I did something like that, I would feel awful. He must really feel awful. I think I will go help him." If that is not my response, then I am bitter, and it is my sin, not his.

I believe that this sin is a major hindrance to revival in this country. When Christians start confessing their sins, they will be able to forgive the sins of others.

Study Guide

Get rid of all bitterness, rage and anger, brawling and slander, along with every form of malice. Be kind and compassionate to one another, forgiving each other, just as in Christ God forgave you. Be imitators of God, therefore, as dearly loved children and live a life of love, just as Christ loved us and gave himself up for us as a fragrant offering and sacrifice to God. (Eph. 4:31–5:2)

Discussion Questions

1. What is bitterness?

2. Is bitterness a sin? Why or why not?

3. Name a situation in your life that caused you to have feelings of bitterness.

4. What is the basis for bitterness? Does it matter the size of the offense?

A characteristic of bitterness is that it remembers details. Of the thousands of situations and conversations that have taken place in our lives, this one is still fresh in our memory. We remember every detail including the words that were used, the intonation and inflection of the voice. This is due to review, review, and more review.

5. What are the world's solutions to getting rid of anger?

   a.

   b.

Realizing we are bitter is the first step to getting rid of our bitterness. The reason people do not deal with bitterness is that they think it is the other person's sin.

6. What does God require us to do with all our bitterness? (James 3:14–15) It is impossible to be compassionate, tenderhearted, and bitter at the same time.

The Next Step: Responding to God's Word

Reflect on a situation where you struggle with bitterness. If you have not surrendered it to the Father, then do so, allowing the grace of Lord Jesus Christ to fill you. Ask for practical steps that you can take, with the help of the Holy Spirit, to resolve this issue. Respond in love by following Christ's law of forgiveness. "Be kind, compassionate to one another, forgiving each other, just as in Christ God forgave you" (Eph. 4:32).

Forgiving Others

Jim Wilson

This is how my heavenly Father will treat each of you unless you forgive your brother from your heart. (Matt. 18:35)

---

*T*he Lord Jesus Christ is speaking here, and He is giving His followers teaching on forgiveness.

Most of us have had experiences when someone has come to us and asked forgiveness. Other times we have gone to ask for forgiveness.

There are several common responses to such requests, but the one you most often hear is, "There is nothing to forgive." This sounds very gracious, but it really is not. It is a means of refusing to forgive. The person you asked to forgive you knows full well that you need forgiving. But still they dodge the request by saying, "Oh, there's nothing to forgive." They may really think there wasn't any problem, but that's not normally the case.

Sometimes they say, "Alright, you are forgiven." They say it because they have to, but that's not what their heart is saying. But the text requires forgiveness from the heart. In other words, God knows who truly forgives, and who does not. We are also told that God is going to treat each of us in a certain way unless we forgive our brothers from the heart. He does not require us to say the right words. Even though you might convince the person in front of you, you will not convince the One who searches the heart. God knows when you have forgiven your brother from your heart. We cannot hide from the Lord when we sin in this way. Our hearts are open and manifest to Him. If we are refusing to forgive, then He knows it. He knows our sin, and He certainly knows the requirements of His word concerning forgiveness.

So what does the Bible teach about how our heavenly Father will treat us? "Then Peter came to Jesus and asked, 'Lord, how many times shall I forgive my brother when he sins against me? Up to seven times?'" (Matt. 18:21). He thought he was asking a virtuous question.

"Jesus answered, 'I tell you, not seven times, but seventy-seven times'" (Matt. 18:22). When Jesus said this, do you think He meant to limit it to seventy-seven? Do we get to count? Are we allowed to keep a record of wrongs?

Anytime someone counts the number of times he has extended forgiveness, there is no true forgiveness. If you forgave your brother from your heart each time he sinned against you, each instance would seem like the first time.

When Jesus teaches about things like turning the other cheek, people misapply it. They say, "Yes, I will let him hit the other cheek, but if he hits me a third time, I am going to deck him."

But when Jesus taught about turning the other cheek, He was teaching us to do it from the heart. Jesus assumes the other person is sinning against you. He assumes the other person is wrong seven times, seventy-seven times, or four hundred and ninety times. But if you are counting, you are not forgiving.

Therefore, the kingdom of heaven is like a king who wanted to settle accounts with his servants. As he began the settlements, a man who owed him ten thousand talents was brought to him. Since he was not able to pay, the master ordered that he and his wife and his children and all that he had be sold to repay the debt.

The servant fell on his knees before him. "Be patient with me," he begged, "and I will pay back everything." The servant's master took pity on him, canceled the debt and let him go.

But when that servant went out he found one of his fellow servants who owed him a hundred denarii. He grabbed him and began to choke him.

"Pay back what you owe me!" he demanded.

His fellow servant fell to his knees and begged him, "Be patient with me and I will pay you back." But he refused. Instead, he went off and had the man thrown into prison until he could pay the debt. When the other servants saw what had happened, they were greatly distressed and went and told their master everything that had happened.

Then the master called the servant in. "You wicked servant," he said, "I canceled all that debt of yours because you begged me to. Shouldn't you have had mercy on your fellow servant just as I had on you?" In anger his master turned him over to the jailers to be tortured, until he should pay back all he owed.

This is how my heavenly Father will treat each of you unless you forgive your brother from your heart. (Matt. 18:23–35)

When we passed from death to life, we were forgiven, and the debt which was eliminated was immense. When we became Christians, we received unconditional forgiveness. It was a gift, and we received it without conditions attached.

There is a difference between conditional forgiveness and unconditional forgiveness. When we were born again, we received unconditional forgiveness. It was a great forgiveness like the forgiveness of the great debt in the parable. Colossians 3:13 says, "Bear with each other and forgive whatever grievances you may have against one another. Forgive as the Lord forgave you." How did the Lord forgive us? Unconditionally, and we are told to forgive as we were forgiven: unconditionally. But suddenly, when it comes to our debtors, we have conditional forgiveness. Remember how the heavenly Father treats those who behave like the wicked servant in the parable.

"Forgive us our debts, as we also have forgiven our debtors" (Matt. 6:12). The Lord instructed us to pray this way. We protest, "God, I don't want to be forgiven this way. If I get forgiven the way I forgive, I'm in big trouble."

The Christian who prays as instructed is praying for conditional forgiveness. In Matthew 6:14, right after the Lord's prayer, Jesus says, "For if you forgive men when they sin against you, your heavenly Father will also forgive you. But if you do not forgive men their sins, your Father will not forgive your sins." Is this true? It is the Lord Jesus who said it.

Someone might object, "How can this be? We have received unconditional forgiveness. Now Jesus is saying that if I forgive men when they sin against me, my heavenly Father will also forgive me, but if I do not forgive men their sins, my Father will not forgive my sins. That sounds like conditional forgiveness to me."

Here is why it's conditional. Jesus said that when we passed from death to life, we were forgiven a great debt. At that time, we had very clear instructions to forgive as we had been forgiven. We were forgiven unconditionally, and we are told to forgive unconditionally.

If someone is forgiving unconditionally, he won't have any problems praying this: "Lord, forgive me as I forgive." This forgiveness will be unconditional. There is no contradiction for the Christian who is doing what he is told. There is only a seeming contradiction when forgiveness is not extended in the same way it is received. That was the problem with the unforgiving servant. He had been forgiven, and he turned around and did not forgive as he had been forgiven.

This is a powerful statement: "This is how my heavenly Father will treat you unless you forgive your brother from your heart, as I forgave you from my heart." If I refuse to forgive, I have good reason to doubt my salvation.

If your brother sins against you, go and show him his fault, just between the two of you. If he listens to you, you have won your brother over. But if he will not listen, take one or two others along, so that "every matter may be established by the testimony of two or three witnesses." If he refuses to listen to them, tell it to the church; and if he refuses to listen even to the church, treat him as you would a pagan or a tax collector. I tell you the truth, whatever you bind on earth will be bound in heaven, and whatever you loose on earth will be loosed in heaven. Again, I tell you that if two of you on earth agree about anything you ask for, it will be done for you by my Father in heaven. For where two or three come together in my name, there am I with them. (Matt. 18:15–20)

This passage, which precedes the parable we have examined, also has to do with heart forgiveness. If your brother sins against you, go and show him his fault just between the two of you. If he listens, you have won your brother over.

"Well, that is not likely to happen. I have tried that. He sinned against me, and I was so mad I went and showed him his faults, and it did not win him over at all." That was because you did not go with forgiveness in your heart. This text does not make sense to many people, because they cannot comprehend going to someone that way. "How can you tell someone who has sinned against you what he's done to you, and expect to win him? He will get defensive." Why will he get defensive? Because someone is accusing him. But if you go with forgiveness in your heart, then the result will not be accusative.

I can guarantee that he will not be won over if his corrector goes with any kind of bitterness, resentment, or an accusative spirit. You must not go to him in that kind of condition. You may only go when there is forgiveness in your heart in advance. That forgiveness cannot be dependent on his repentance. I can guarantee he will not be repentant if he is not approached with forgiveness. We must go with love and forgiveness. If he listens, we have won our brother over.

If he will not listen even though he has been approached this way, we are to take one or two others along, people who also have forgiveness in their hearts.

This is not what normally happens. Someone goes with an accusation, and the recipient gets defensive. So two other people with one side of the story are collected, and they come and back up the initial corrector. They are not successful, either.

Everyone must have forgiveness in his heart so that if the offender refuses to repent, it is obviously his problem. If he refuses to listen, the church must be told. Of course, it is also necessary for the church to be full of forgiveness.

There are churches that think they exercise godly church discipline. They do not, because they lack this attitude. They go to this guy, lay it on him, and he refuses it. They get two or three others, lay it on him, and he refuses them, too. Then the church kicks him out, but there is no forgiveness in their hearts. However, one of the primary objectives of church discipline is to restore the offender.

If he refuses to listen to the church, he is to be treated as a pagan or a tax collector. I do not believe the Lord Jesus meant as pagans or tax collectors were actually treated. I think he means as pagans and tax collectors should be treated. In Matthew 5, Jesus tells us to treat the just and the unjust as the Father does— equitably. He tells us to love our enemies. That means that when we treat them as pagans and tax collectors, it is loving treatment. It merely means that they are considered outside the fellowship, but with love and forgiveness from the heart. The only problem is that they don't want the forgiveness which the godly are extending to them from their hearts. It is because of this teaching that Peter asked the question which led to the parable you just read: "How many times should I forgive my brother?"

"Love...keeps no record of wrongs" (1 Cor. 13:4–5). Love does not keep score. You may have heard a husband or wife say, "You always do this, and you never do that." What does that mean? Someone is keeping score. The Bible says to never do this. A record of wrongs is only kept when someone is adding up the offenses. Forgiveness does not do that.

What did Jesus mean when He said, "Whatever you bind on earth will be bound in heaven"? Many Christians use the verse about two or three agreeing on anything out of context. The verse has to do with church discipline and forgiving your brother. It is right between the story Jesus told about forgiveness and Peter's question about how many times he had to forgive. When two or three gather together in His name, the Lord Jesus Christ is with them. This has to do with decisions about forgiving others who have sinned against you. Jesus was speaking of Christian churches, full of forgiveness, that are acting in His name. They are acting how He told them to act. Then when they make a decision based upon His word, He honors it.

He does not honor the decision because the church plugs a church-discipline formula. But if they are acting with the character and the love of the Lord Jesus

Christ, when the body of forgiving believers makes a decision to discipline someone who is not willing to repent, God honors it in heaven.

You can see the relationship between this and bitterness. Bitterness is really unforgiveness. It is saying that someone did something to me, and I am not going to forgive him. Of course bitterness does not think of itself as sin; it can only see the sin of the other person.

In one sense, forgiveness is unilateral. In one sense, Jesus Christ forgave us all before we repented. The forgiveness did not become active until we received it. But God was not up in heaven holding a grudge until we got around to repenting. He is not up there bitter until we repent. He has forgiveness in His heart before we appropriate it. God has unilateral forgiveness, and He requires us to have unilateral forgiveness toward anyone who ever sins against us. We think of what the other person did to us, or said to us, and really the issue has nothing to do with what the other person did or said.

When a Christian has forgiveness from the heart, he is not concerned about himself. He is concerned about the person who did the sinning against him. We tend to be like Peter: "Sure, Lord, I'll forgive him seven times, but if he goes to eight, he's in real trouble." But real forgiveness doesn't keep count. If you have a tendency to keep count within or without the family, it is very likely that you are not forgiving. Jesus said that His heavenly Father will treat each of us with the same lack of forgiveness unless we forgive from the heart. Forgive your brother from your heart.

"I do not have forgiveness in my heart." Then who needs forgiving? The one who needs forgiving is the one who has this unlove, this hatred, this bad attitude, this grudge, or whatever. You cannot have it both ways. You cannot have unforgiveness in your heart and rejoice in the Lord.

It is possible to have unforgiveness in your heart and still go to church and sing. But it is all a fake! The singing is false. You can make people sing, but when people are clean you don't have to make them sing. People will spontaneously sing from a full heart. Why? Because they have clean hearts.

There is a big difference between singing because you are rejoicing in the Lord, and singing to get joy. Some Christians go to church every Sunday and sing to get joy. The joy ends when they quit singing, because there is uncleanness in their heart.

We would all like to think that we are the good guy and the other person has the problem. It might not be true. Assume you are the one who has the problem of lack of forgiveness. If a Christian has forgiveness in his heart, he will rejoice regardless of how wrong the other person is or how greatly the other person sins against him.

How can you show forgiveness to someone when you have to be very firm because you don't believe in their lifestyle? It is not really that difficult. If you have forgiveness in your heart, they will know it, regardless of how firm you are. They will know it based upon your tone. People can tell when you love them. They can tell when you are being firm because you are bitter, and they can tell when you do it out of love. The only thing you have to be sure of is your attitude in the conversation. You do not have to worry how they will take it. The results are the Lord's. They may not accept it, but they do know the difference.

Periodically, I have had to be very firm with people. One time, many decades ago, a man had just gotten right with the Lord the previous March. He had been a Christian since his sophomore year in college, but in his senior year he really got right with the Lord. He asked to live with us in our home through the summer after graduation. We shifted the kids around, and he moved all his stuff into our house in June.

My wife was putting the kids in bed, and we were down in the living room. I asked him how things were going. He said, "Not so good."

"Is it the same problem you had before?"

He said, "Yes."

"Same girl?"

He said it was the same girl.

I asked if he remembered how wonderfully God forgave him in March?

He said, "It was wonderful. There was great joy and peace."

I said, "Well, He can do it again. Let's pray right now. You may repent and confess, and be restored."

He said, "No."

I said, "It's true."

"Yeah, I know. I've seen it happen. I know He will do it again, but I am not quite ready."

I said, "I do not think you understand. You do not have an option. You know better. You have to be restored now."

"No; I will do it sometime, but not now."

"I think I will have to tell the church that you are living in sin."

"You would tell the church what I told you in confidence?"

"I did not know it was in confidence, and I didn't know what you were going to tell me, and I didn't know you were going to be unrepentant having told me. God tells me to take it to the church because we are not to have fellowship with you. We are not going to eat with you. The Bible tells us what to do with anyone who calls himself a brother who is a fornicator. The church is not very godly, so they will probably kick me out for gossiping. Nevertheless, the Bible tells me to tell the church. I will also tell the Officers' Christian Union, and they will not bat an eye. They will remove you so fast it will not be funny."

He got angry.

I told him there was one other problem. "In 1 Corinthians 5, it says we are not to eat with you. We are not allowed to keep company with immoral people who call themselves believers. If anybody calls himself a brother and lives this way, we may not even eat with him. You want me to disobey God because you are going to be unrepentant. You want me to eat with you and have fellowship with you while you stay unrepentant. You have already moved your stuff in, so you can stay overnight. But if you're not right with the Lord by morning, I want you out of this house before breakfast, and I don't want you to speak to my wife or children."

He got very angry.

I said, "I love you very much. You know I love you very much. You may stay here all summer in fellowship, but you do not eat breakfast here in the morning unless you are in fellowship."

He knew I loved him and that I wasn't holding a grudge against him. He knew the love was real. But if the same thing had been said with any kind of bitter malice, it would have been wrong. He was right with God by breakfast, and he stayed there all summer.

Forgiveness is not inconsistent with godly discipline. If there is discipline, it does not mean that there is a lack of forgiveness.

Spend time with God alone and clean house. If you have any unforgiveness toward anyone else, forgive him from the heart. God is very quick to take you up on any serious business with Him. He is quick to forgive.

Study Guide

Then Peter came to Jesus and asked, "Lord, how many times shall I forgive my brother when he sins against me? Up to seven times?" Jesus answered, "I tell you, not seven times, but seventy-seven times." (Matt. 18:21–22)

Discussion Questions

1. Describe a situation when someone has committed a sin against you and then asked for your forgiveness. Were you able to forgive this person from your heart?

2. Describe a situation when someone has committed a sin against you repeatedly and then asked your forgiveness. Were you able to forgive this person from your heart?

   Peter asked Jesus if seven was enough times to forgive someone. Jesus answered, "Seventy-seven times," meaning that we should not keep track of how many times we forgive someone. If we did, and it was seven times in a day, then we would be tempted not to forgive. We should always forgive those who say they are repentant, no matter how many times they ask. We must not judge whether he is truly repentant. "If your brother sins, rebuke him, and if he repents, forgive him" (Luke 17:3).

3. What does the parable of the unforgiving debtor teach us about conditional versus unconditional forgiveness?

4. Jesus teaches us how to pray in Matthew 6:5–15. What is the one condition He places on our forgiveness in verses fourteen and fifteen?

5. What are Jesus' guidelines for dealing with those who sin against us? Who were these guidelines meant for? (Matt. 18:15–20)

   Forgiveness is not to be dependent on the offender's repentance. He will not be repentant if he is not approached with forgiveness from the heart.

6. What does Jesus teach us about those who refuse to listen even to the church? How does this relate to bitterness?

   When a Christian has forgiveness from the heart, he is concerned about the person who did the sinning against him. He is not concerned about himself.

The Next Step: Responding to God's Word

1 Corinthians 13:4–5 states that "Love . . . keeps no record of wrongs." Love does not keep score. If there are people in your life with whom you keep score, surrender your score card to God. Ask for God's forgiveness so that you may come to understand His mercy. Then respond to God's calling to forgive from the heart.

Man's Anger

Heather Wilson Torosyan

Then the Lord said to Cain, "Why are you angry? Why is your face downcast? If you do what is right, will you not be accepted?" (Gen. 4:6–7a)

Someone has just crunched your car, and you are angry. He was sixteen and hot-rodding. You are angry at the kid, at all of today's kids, and at the system for letting such irresponsible people out on the streets. And to top it off some Christian comes up and tells you to put away all anger and wrath. Well, that really does it. Platitudes! That's easy for him to say. Besides, the Bible says you can get angry. Jesus got angry when he drove the money changers out of the temple. And anyway, it's bad for you to keep anger in; it is better to be authentic than hypocritical.

On and on go the excuses and justifications. You attempt to convince yourself that it was really okay to get angry. I suspect we have all heard and very likely used these excuses. If anybody is so foolish as to try to point out that angry is not what God would have us to be, we simply add him to the reasons for being angry.

Some people lose their tempers over what you may call trifling things (i.e. those things that don't bother you): inefficiency in the office, someone cutting in quickly and taking a parking place, the way a husband leaves his socks on the floor, or the wife who is chronically late. Isn't it amazing what can make people really ticked?

Others may get angry at "more righteous" things like world hunger, abortion, war, lack of civil rights, or discrimination. There are hosts of other reasons that can set off tempers, reasons that are as individual as fingerprints. But whatever our trigger is, the Bible has some very definite things to say about anger.

The most often used justification is "The Bible says to get angry." Well, yes, as a matter of fact, it does say, "Be angry..." (Eph. 4:26). But that is often where people stop. They ignore the next part that says, "and do not sin." Christians are often very good on the first part of the command, but a trifle weak on the second half. The verse adds a second condition to the command: "Do not let the sun go down on your anger."

There are other verses that can be interpreted to allow anger. "Everyone should be quick to listen, slow to speak and slow to become angry..." Again, that indicates that as long as you don't fly off the handle, that's okay. But again, the following phrase adds some light to the subject. "For man's anger does not bring about the righteous life that God desires" (James 1:19–20).

Perhaps, then, it is okay to be angry if

- We do not sin.
- We don't go to sleep with it.
- It is anger from God and not man's anger.
- It achieves righteousness.
- It comes slowly.

Do you get the feeling that if these qualifications are met, the amount of anger would be cut drastically?

Another biblical reference that is appealed to is when Jesus cleansed the temple (Matt. 21, John 2). This is a tricky passage to use as a proof text, for our anger is rarely so righteous. Even though the passage never actually says that Jesus was angry, we can still see how it fits at least four of the five qualifications. The anger seemed to be God's, for the cause of the anger was not self-centered. Jesus was purging God's temple. The result was righteousness. Because it was of God, it was not sin. It came slowly enough to allow Him to make a whip. If we like, we can assume the sun did not go down on His anger.

If we are not up to likening our anger to Christ's, we may well use the "you don't understand" routine. Perhaps I don't understand, but Christ certainly does. "For we do not have a high priest who is unable to sympathize with our weaknesses, but we have one who has been tempted in every way, just as we are, yet was without sin" (Heb. 4:15). Christ sympathizes with our weakness, but it doesn't end there; He gives us grace in time of need (v. 16).

If we were more sophisticated, we could say that psychologically it is better to release our anger. Pent-up anger may give us ulcers. Of course, if we release our anger, others may get ulcers. It rarely occurs to people that there is a third option, i.e., taking our anger to God. This does not mean venting our spleen towards God ("authenticity"). It means admitting to God that you are angry and that if it is not going to achieve His righteousness, you do not want it. With this confession, our anger is removed from us, we may continue our life in the joy of the Lord, and nobody gets ulcers.

The Scriptures have just these few indications that anger may be alright under limited circumstances, but it says a lot more about the folly of anger and its sinfulness. "But now you must rid yourselves of all such things as these: anger, rage, malice, slander, and filthy language from your lips" (Col. 3:8). "Fits of rage" is listed as one of the deeds of the flesh in Galatians 5:20. "An angry man stirs up dissention, and a hot-tempered one commits many sins" (Prov. 29:22) "A quick-tempered man displays folly" (Prov. 14:29). Proverbs has a lot to say on the subject.

Suppose you are convinced that your anger is not of God, and you would like to get rid of it. How do you start?

First, it is good to see where your anger is from: "The good man brings good things out of the good stored up in his heart, and the evil man brings evil things out of the evil stored up in his heart. For out of the overflow of his heart his mouth speaks" (Luke 6:45). What we see here is that the fruit of our lives is generated from the state of our heart. If our heart has an evil treasure, the overflow will be evil.

If that is the case, two steps must be taken. The first is expressed in Psalm 139:23–24: "Search me, O God, and know my heart; test me and know my anxious thoughts. See if there is any offensive way in me, and lead me in the way everlasting." We need a heart-searching by God.

The second step is to confess the sins of the heart to God. "But if we walk in the light, as he is in the light, we have fellowship with one another, and the blood of Jesus, his Son, purifies us from all sin . . . . If we confess our sins, he is faithful and just and will forgive us our sins and purify us from all unrighteousness" (1 John 1:7, 9). The anger will disappear from our hearts like the money changers from the temple.

Once our heart is clean, we should fill it with all sorts of good things. Things that are true, honorable, right, pure, lovely, of good repute, excellent, and worthy of praise are a few suggestions given by Paul in Philippians 4:8. This can also be defined as the renewing of your mind (Rom. 12:2).

Does the idea of putting away all anger seem hopelessly impossible to you? If it were only up to us to keep perfect control, the idea would be impossible. But thank Him it is not. "To him who is able to keep you from falling and to present you before his glorious presence without fault and with great joy . . . . Amen" (Jude 24).

Note: In an age where there is so much talk about low self-love, it does not occur to people that someone might love himself too much. Most anger is not generated in protection of other people. It is a response caused by loving yourself too much. "I am too nice or too important to be treated this way." Therefore, anger. If the anger is a fit of rage, it is a characteristic of a non-Christian. Jesus saves us out of the list of works of the flesh in Galatians 5:19–21 and saves us into the fruit of the Spirit in Galatians 5:22–23. If you know you are a Christian and have "fits of rage," these must be confessed and forsaken today.

Jim Wilson

Study Guide

Then the Lord said to Cain, "Why are you angry? Why is your face downcast? If you do what is right, will you not be accepted?" (Gen. 4:6–7a)

Discussion Questions

1. How can someone tell when you are angry?

2. Describe the last time you became really angry.

3. What does Ephesians 4:26 say about anger?

   For man's anger does not bring about the righteous life that God desires. (James 1:20)

4. What does God say about the folly of anger and its sinfulness?

   Colossians 3:8
   Galatians 5:20
   Proverbs 29:22
   Proverbs 14:29

5. Where does your anger come from?

The good man brings good things out of the good stored up in his heart, and the evil man brings evil things out of the evil stored up in his heart. For out of the overflow of his heart his mouth speaks. (Luke 6:45)

6. The fruit of our lives is generated from the state of our heart. If our heart has an evil treasure, the overflow will be evil. What two steps must be taken if you would like to get rid of your anger?Step One: Step Two:

The Next Step: Responding to God's Word

If we are willing to give up our anger to God and confess our sins, God promises to create in us a clean heart. Reflect on how you deal with anger. Ask God to search your heart and thoughts, revealing any offensive way in you. Respond by letting God take control so that He can "lead me in the way everlasting" (Psalm 139:24).

Fits of Rage

Jim Wilson

The acts of the sinful nature are obvious: sexual immorality, impurity and debauchery; idolatry and witchcraft; hatred, discord, jealousy, fits of rage, selfish ambition, dissensions, factions and envy; drunkenness, orgies, and the like. I warn you, as I did before, that those who live like this will not inherit the kingdom of God. (Gal. 5:19–21)

But the fruit of the Spirit is love, joy, peace, patience, kindness, goodness, faithfulness, gentleness and self control. Against such things there is no law. Those who belong to Christ Jesus have crucified the sinful nature with its passions and desires. Since we live by the Spirit, let us keep in step with the Spirit. (Gal. 5:22–25)

---

9 have been a witness to several very scary fits of rage. One time I went to confront a pastor who was being unfaithful. He had come to his wife's mobile home to visit his teenage daughters. He did not respond to me in anger, but immediately afterward went into a fit of rage with his wife and one daughter. When he left, he was still so dangerous I locked the door. He came back and pounded on the door very hard and then began to rock the trailer. He married the other woman. Ten years later he repented.

Many years ago, Bessie and I went together hoping to reconcile a married couple. The "other woman" was there. This other woman went berserk. No one was hurt. She took it out on the car. She was not a Christian.

Another time, a man came into my bookstore to inform me, in a fit of rage, that he was going to kill his wife. We managed to hide his wife until the fit of rage was over. He was not a Christian.

A "fit of rage" is an act of the sinful nature. We see it clearly in very young children. We call it a tantrum. As the child gets older, we might say in a tormenting way, "Temper, temper, temper!" This does not normally moderate the explosion. Other expressions that describe fits of rage are "losing it" and "going ballistic." These euphemisms for fits of rage are descriptive, but do not sound as sinful.

"Short fuse" is another euphemism for a person who is quick to anger. All of us know people like that. Some people take pride in having a short fuse. Their friends and relatives have learned how to walk softly or to give them a wide berth. These people terrorize their families or hold them hostage to their anger, which might erupt any time.

The opposite of the acts of the sinful nature is the fruit of the Spirit. It is easy to see that self-control is the opposite of a fit of rage. But it is not the only opposite. A person in a fit of rage is not loving, joyful, peaceful, patient, kind, good, faithful, or gentle. A fit of rage undoes all the fruit of the Spirit. This is why it is natural for a person not born of the Spirit.

If someone is born of the Spirit, a fit of rage is neither normal nor acceptable. So why do Christians lose their tempers? If they are truly Christians, they have accumulated many little sins which they have not repented of, not confessed, and consequently not received forgiveness for. This leaves them ready to give in to a little temptation with a big fit of rage. David describes the buildup this way: "Keep your servant also from willful sins; may they not rule over me. Then will I be blameless, innocent of great transgression" (Psalm 19:13). Notice that the description is one of prevention. The Christian who is given to fits of rage has not been eager to be kept from willful sins. He has allowed them to rule over him. Then he ends up guilty of great transgression.

It is not possible to prevent fits of rage without complete confession and repentance of all your previous fits of rage. This confession must be made without any euphemisms to minimize the sin, and it must also include the willful sins that led up to the fits of rage.

"Since, then, you have been raised with Christ, set your hearts on things above, where Christ is seated at the right hand of God. Set your minds on things above, not on earthly things. For you died, and your life is now hidden with Christ in God. When Christ, who is your life, appears, then you also will appear with him in glory" (Col. 3:1–4). This instruction is foundational for the prevention of rage, anger, and any other sins that cling so closely. It only works if you are a Christian, because only a Christian can obey it.

Once our hearts and minds are in the right place with Christ, we are given this instruction: "But now you must rid yourselves of all such things as these: anger, rage, malice, slander, and filthy language from your lips" (Col. 3:8).

This command is not given to those who are not children of God. That does not mean that these things are permissible for unbelievers; it means that the unbelievers cannot possibly obey the command to rid themselves of them. They can express anger and rage, but they cannot get rid of anger and rage without repentance. The unbeliever needs to repent of his sins to God, confess that Jesus Christ is Lord, and believe in his heart that Christ died for his sins and rose from the dead.

He told them, "This is what is written: The Messiah will suffer and rise from the dead on the third day, and repentance for the forgiveness of sins will be preached in his name to all nations, beginning at Jerusalem." (Luke 24:46–47)

If you declare with your mouth, "Jesus is Lord," and believe in your heart that God raised him from the dead, you will be saved. (Rom. 10:9)

Study Guide

The acts of the sinful nature are obvious: sexual immorality, impurity and debauchery; idolatry and witchcraft; hatred, discord, jealousy, fits of rage, selfish ambition, dissensions, factions and envy; drunkenness, orgies, and the like. I warn you, as I did before, that those who live like this will not inherit the kingdom of God. (Gal. 5:19–21)

Discussion Questions

1. Galatians 5:19–21 provides us with a list of vices that hinder us from developing a closer relationship with the Lord. There is a phrase that says, "those that live like this." That is a statement of normality. If fits of rage or any of the other sins in the list are normal for you, you will not inherit the kingdom of God. What vices are hindering you?

2. If we belong to Jesus Christ, what have we done with the sinful nature (Gal. 5:24)?

   A fit of rage is an act of the sinful nature. We may call it a temper tantrum in children and "losing it" or "going ballistic" as we get older. These euphemisms are descriptive, but they do not change the fact that this is sin. It is an act that is normal for non-Christians. It is not acceptable or normal for Christians. If the first list (Gal. 5:19–21) describes you better, then you have every reason to believe you are not in Christ. Jesus Christ does a better job of saving than that. If you are in both lists, then it is imperative that you get out of the first list by confessing and forsaking.

3. What topic or situation seems to push your button every time it happens?

4. What can we do to prevent fits of rage from building inside us (Psalm 19:12–13)?

5. Colossians 3:8 commands us to rid ourselves of what things?

6. Colossians 3:9 gives the "why" and the "how." What are they?

7. There is a difference between indicative statements and imperatives. Indicative is what is. An imperative is a command to do. Is Galatians 5:24 an indicative or an imperative?

Once we crucify our evil desires, the Holy Spirit can produce in us the character traits that are found in the nature of Christ. (Gal. 5:22–23)

The Next Step: Responding to God's Word

Reflect on areas in your life that hinder the Holy Spirit from working in you. Respond by letting God take control. "Remain in me, and I will remain in you. No branch can bear fruit by itself; it must remain in the vine. Neither can you bear fruit unless you remain in me" (John 15:4).

Taking Offense

Heather Wilson Torosyan

Love is...not easily angered, it keeps no record of wrongs. (1 Cor. 13:4–5)

---

*W*e know from James' epistle that if a man can control his tongue he is well-nigh perfect, capable of controlling his whole body. The difficulty is that there are so many imperfect people who have not yet learned to bridle the tongue. In the meanwhile, people are being hurt right and left by what other people say.

It is not only the tongue that can hurt, but also the actions. So not only must all our friends and acquaintances bridle their tongues; they must likewise apply this know-how to their bodies.

For some reason, we put all responsibility on the offender rather than the offended. I have no intention of excusing an uncontrolled tongue. The tongue must be controlled. But until it is, do I have a right to be hurt? Must I remain susceptible to hurt feelings until everyone else is perfect? It seems to me the less efficient of two ways to achieve the same result.

We would like to have people be so nice to us all the time that there would never be an occasion for us to be hurt. Obviously, this is unrealistic, so what I am suggesting is that the offended toughen up.[2]

One way to do this is by looking at the example of Christ. "He was despised and forsaken of men, a man of sorrows, acquainted with grief, and like one from whom men hide their face. He was despised, and we did not esteem Him . . . . He was oppressed and He was afflicted, yet He did not open His mouth" (Is. 53:3, 9). Any of us in this same position would consider that we had every right to be hurt. If that's the way they are going to be, see if I'm ever going to 1) speak to them again, 2) be nice to them again, 3) forgive them, or 4) die for them. Yet if this had been our Lord's reaction, He would never have gone to the cross. Granted, this was

---

2 "Toughen up" does not mean to build a wall or some other defense mechanism to keep from getting hurt. That does not work; that only makes you become hard and calloused. It does mean to follow Jesus as an example, as in 1 Peter 2:21. Jesus stayed vulnerable. The best way to keep from getting hurt is to follow Jesus and stay vulnerable. That person stays soft. He does not become hardened. The best way to "toughen up" is to stay open and take it. It hurts less. - J.W.

an exceptional case. He did have all the power of God at His disposal. He is perfect, and we are not.

> Have this attitude in yourselves which was also in Christ Jesus who, although He existed in the form of God, did not regard equality with God a thing to be grasped, but emptied Himself, taking the form of a bond servant and being made in the likeness of men. And being found in appearance as a man, He humbled Himself by becoming obedient to the point of death, even death on a cross. (Phil. 2:5–8)

We should have a like mind to Christ in these four aspects:

- Don't grasp onto your identity or your rights.
- Empty yourself.
- Be a servant.
- Be humble.

With such an attitude, we can also endure all sorts of crosses for the joy that awaits on the other side, thinking nothing of the shame attached (Heb. 12:2).

Normally those closest to us are the ones who can hurt us the most. A stranger has much less capacity for hurting us than a husband, wife, friend, brother, or sister. When wounded by someone close, we tell ourselves, "If he really loved me, he wouldn't say that." But analyzing this statement reveals whom we are really thinking about. Are we thinking about the lack of love in the other person and how he needs help? No, we are thinking how his lack of love affects us. In other words, we are conceited—thinking about self and how everyone else's action relates to us.

A very favorite passage on love is 1 Corinthians 13. It says love is "not self-seeking, it is not easily angered, it keeps no record of wrongs."

When we feel hurt, it is because there is no ready forgiveness in our hearts. Forgiveness, by nature, does not keep a record of wrongs. In Ephesians 4:32, a well-known but rarely practiced verse, Paul tells us to "be kind and compassionate to one another, forgiving each other, just as in Christ God forgave you." We must forgive as we have been forgiven. Remember 70 x 7. There is no limit to the command, and certainly none to the Lord's ability to forgive.

Considering that for every temptation the Lord provides a way of escape, there is no reason any of us should ever be hurt again. That sounds like a tall order, I know, and many would say it is impossible. But it is my belief that if the Lord promised a way of escape, each time it will be there.

Study Guide

He was despised and rejected by men, a man of sorrows, and familiar with suffering. Like one from whom men hide their faces he was despised, and we esteemed him not...He was oppressed and afflicted, yet he did not open his mouth; he was led like a lamb to the slaughter, and as a sheep before her shearers is silent, so he did not open his mouth. (Isa. 53:3, 7)

Discussion Questions

1. Describe a time when you were accused and punished for something you did not do.

2. Did you become bitter or better because of this experience?

3. How is it possible to be like-minded with Christ when someone has wronged you (Phil. 2:5–8)?

4. List the characteristics of love (1 Cor. 13:4–5).

   When we feel hurt, it is because there is no ready forgiveness in our hearts.

5. How are we asked to deal with those who hurt us (Rom. 12:17–21)?

The Next Step: Responding to God's Word

Reflect on God's instructions in 1 Corinthians 13:4–5. Love is patient, love is kind. It does not envy, it does not boast, it is not proud. It is not rude, it is not self-seeking, it is not easily angered, it keeps no record of wrongs. If we are to be imitators of Christ, then we must ask God to fill us with His strength and grace, enabling us to forgive from the heart. Respond to those who offend you with the same compassion and forgiveness God gives you.

Bridling the Tongue

Chris Vlachos

All kinds of animals, birds, reptiles and sea creatures are being tamed and have been tamed by mankind, but no human being can tame the tongue. It is a restless evil, full of deadly poison. (James 3:7–8)

Some time ago, a magnetic storm occurred in New York state that caused a conversation on a telephone line to interfere with the radio waves emitted from a nearby radio station. As a result, the conversation was broadcast on the radio without the knowledge of the two talkers. It was a coast-to-coast program!

All of us have been guilty of gossip at one time or another. In fact, there is enough gossip in many a church to make the recording angel weep as he records it. It is a sinful practice which God takes seriously and wants us to stop.

Paul speaks of gossip in 1 Timothy 3:11: "Women must likewise be dignified, not malicious gossips, but temperate, faithful in all things." Lest we think that men are immune to this disease, Paul similarly addresses them in his second letter to Timothy, predicting that in the last days men will be, "unloving, irreconcilable, malicious gossips, without self-control, brutal, haters of good" (2 Tim. 3:3). The Greek word which Paul uses in these two instances is the word *diabolos*, from which we derive our word "devil." We don't need to consult our calendar of saints to know who the patron saint of gossip is! A gossiper is nothing more than "the devil's mailman."

Diabolos is also at times translated "slanderer." Gossip is slander. In 2 Timothy 3, Paul places gossip in the middle of a list of other vicious practices. Clearly, the serious nature of gossip is indicated.

Unfortunately, it is often difficult to detect gossip/slander in ourselves. How can we know if we are gossips? There are four questions to ask ourselves when we are tempted to share information concerning someone else. The answers to these questions will likely indicate whether or not we are gossiping/slandering.

1. *Why am I saying this?* Is my real motive to criticize? Am I really out to help the person about whom I am speaking, or is my goal to hurt them? Often under

the guise of sharing a prayer request we are really gossiping. We often rationalize our gossip when our real aim is to put the other person down in order to cast ourselves in a better light. Be careful how you answer this first question. If you catch yourself trying to justify or to excuse something negative that you are about to say concerning someone, you are probably on the threshold of slander.

2. *Is it possible that there is another side to the story?* Webster defines gossip as "spreading rumors." A rumor is an unauthenticated story. If our story is unauthenticated, we are gossiping. It has been said that it isn't the people who tell all they know that cause most of the trouble in the church, it is the ones who tell more than they know.

3. *Would I feel comfortable saying this to Jesus?* How would He answer us after we shared with Him some negative information concerning another? Very likely He would respond by asking us what relevance the information has to our following Him (John 21:22). If you wouldn't be comfortable sharing the tale with the Lord, then the information is probably unsuitable to share with anyone else.

4. *Am I building up the person I'm speaking to by sharing this?* Charles Spurgeon once said that gossip "emits a three-fold poison; it injures the teller, the hearer, and the person concerning whom the tale is told." We should be very careful to heed Paul's

exhortation: "Do not let any unwholesome talk come out of your mouths, but only what is helpful for building others up according to their needs, that it may benefit those who listen" (Eph. 4:29).

The answers to these four questions will help us to detect gossip/slander. If after asking yourself these questions, you are still not sure if what you are about to share is gossip, then don't say it. Is it really necessary that you do?

One last thought: How can we stop this sinful habit of gossiping that not only plagues our lives but invades and destroys churches? The cure for gossip is twofold. First, don't spread it. Gossip is something that goes in one ear and out the mouth. Bridle your tongue! If you can't say anything good about somebody, then don't say anything at all. Second, don't listen to it! You can't have gossiping tongues unless there are gossiping ears. Don't encourage the gossiper. Don't be quick to believe what is said. Steer the conversation to a discussion of the person's good points. Nothing will more quickly stop the gossiper/slanderer than doing this.

It has been said that gossip has neither legs or wings but is composed entirely of "tales." Sadly, most of these tales sting and have a poisonous effect on the work of revival in a life or a church. Although we are bothered from time to time by wasps in the sanctuary, may this diabolical pest, gossip, become extinct in our churches.

"Finally, brothers, whatever is true, whatever is noble, whatever is right, whatever is pure, whatever is lovely, whatever is admirable—if anything is excellent or praiseworthy—think about such things" (Phil. 4:8).

Study Guide

But mark this: There will be terrible times in the last days. People will be lovers of themselves, lovers of money, boastful, proud, abusive, disobedient to their parents, ungrateful, unholy, without love, unforgiving, slanderous, without self-control, brutal, not lovers of good, treacherous, rash, conceited, lovers of pleasure rather than lovers of God. (2 Tim. 3:3–4)

Discussion Questions

1. What does Ephesians 4:29 have to say about gossip?

2. Paul speaks of malicious gossip in 1 Timothy 3:11 and 2 Timothy 3:3. What is the definition for each of these words?

Malicious:

Gossip:

3. Who is the patron saint of gossip?

4. List four questions we can ask ourselves when we are tempted to share information concerning another person.

5. What is Paul's cure for gossip and other forms of malice (Eph. 4:31–32)?

The Next Step: Responding to God's Word

God asks us to set aside time to meet with Him each day. Ask Him to renew your mind, refresh your spirit, and provide you with the strength needed to be like-minded with Christ. Then respond by allowing God's love to guide what you say and how you think. "May the words of my mouth and the meditation of my heart be pleasing in your sight, O Lord, my Rock and my Redeemer" (Psalm 19:14).

Introspection

Jim Wilson

But if we walk in the light, as he is in the light, we have fellowship with one another, and the blood of Jesus, his Son, purifies us from all sin. (1 John 1:7)

Introspection is the act or practice of meditating on our own past actions and emotions. This meditation brings these things to our attention, and we focus on them and evaluate ourselves in the light of our flickering meditative candle. Because many people consider our past (either distant or recent) to be the cause or explanation of our present actions and emotions, introspection is often encouraged. Even where it is not encouraged by others, it is practiced regularly by many Christians.

Introspection is not like walking in the sunlight on a summer day. Instead, it is like going down dungeon steps with a sputtering candle in your hand. The tiny light throws long shadows and dimly shows up skeletons, spider webs, and gross, crawly things. These are the things in our past which have been done to us or which we have done and are ashamed of. They include our imagination.

A person who is addicted to introspection keeps going deeper into this dead dungeon or inspects the same skeletons over and over again. The candle is not a very good light and never provides a solution to his awful, macabre past. The fascination with this subject matter is never a source of joy. It is a cause of depression. It is probably the primary cause of depression in people with melancholic, perfectionist personalities.

THE CONVICTION OF THE JUDGE

Introspection says things like "How awful!" "How gross!" "The Lord won't have me now." "If I were God, I would not forgive me." Introspection is a downer, not an upper. It is accusative, not convicting.

In a court of law, there is a difference between the accuser and the convicter. The accuser is the prosecuting attorney, and the convicter is the judge. The prosecuting attorney seeks to prove guilt, and the judge decides if it has been proven. Once the judge makes his decision, the trial is over. However, the prosecutor will continue to say the person is guilty even if the judge says he is not.

In the Bible, Satan is the accuser. The Holy Spirit is the convicter.

THE PERFECT LIGHT

The alternative to introspection and its negative results is found in 1 John 1:5–10. I will quote verses 5 and 7: "This is the message we have heard from him and declare to you: God is light; in him there is no darkness at all . . . . But if we walk in the light, as he is in the light, we have fellowship with one another, and the blood of Jesus, his Son, purifies us from all sin."

This light is the source of all light. It is not a candle flickering in the darkness. There are no shadows. James 1:17 says: "Every good and perfect gift is from above, coming down from the Father of the heavenly lights, who does not change like shifting shadows."

Given that this light is complete, if we walk in it, nothing is hidden. Sin is shown in convicting power as opposed to accusing power. The sin is forgiven immediately, because the blood of Jesus keeps on cleansing. Fellowship is normal, because we are in the light, and we are made clean continually. Obedience is a natural result of the conviction and cleansing.

There is a wonderful example of this kind of conviction-cleansing-fellowship-obedience in Isaiah 6:1–8:

In the year that King Uzziah died, I saw the Lord seated on a throne, high and exalted, and the train of his robe filled the temple. Above him were seraphs, each with six wings: With two wings they covered their faces, with two they covered their feet, and with two they were flying. And they were calling to one another: "Holy, holy, holy is the LORD Almighty; the whole earth is full of his glory." At the sound of their voices the doorposts and thresholds shook and the temple was filled with smoke.

"Woe to me!" I cried. "I am ruined! For I am a man of unclean lips, and I live among a people of unclean lips, and my eyes have seen the King, the LORD Almighty."

Then one of the seraphs flew to me with a live coal in his hand, which he had taken with tongs from the altar. With it he touched my mouth and said, "See, this has touched your lips; your guilt is taken away and your sin atoned for."

Then I heard the voice of the Lord saying, "Whom shall I send? And who will go for us?"

And I said, "Here am I. Send me!"

It was not introspection that made Isaiah conscious of his sin; it was being in the presence of God. He was in the light. He could not keep quiet about his sin; he could not hide. As soon as he confessed his sin, he was forgiven. As soon as he was forgiven, he was ready to be obedient.

You may say that you have never been forgiven that fast. Perhaps you've felt that way because of the accuser instead of the convicter/cleanser. The accuser does not want anyone to be forgiven.

WALKING IN THE LIGHT

Next time you find yourself tending towards introspection, refuse to do it. Instead, come to the light. How? Pray Psalm 139:23–24: "Search me, O God, and know my heart; test me and know my anxious thoughts. See if there is any offensive way in me, and lead me in the way everlasting."

Look up, not in. You do not have to look for sin. You will find sin much more quickly, starkly, and with a solution attached if you come to God and the completed work of Jesus Christ.

Study Guide

Sin forgiven is not the same as sin suppressed. Introspection seeks to remember in detail the sins of the past and tends to worry about the future. Paul said, "Forgetting what is behind and straining toward what is ahead, I press on toward the goal to win the prize for which God has called me heavenward in Christ Jesus." Jesus said, "Therefore do not worry about tomorrow, for tomorrow will worry about itself. Each day has enough trouble of its own." Forgetting the past is not suppression of sin if the past has been forgiven.

Walking in the light is a present-tense activity. It does not dwell in the past or in the future. It listens to the convicter, not the accuser. It receives cleansing and responds with obedience. "Search me, O God, and know my heart; test me and know my anxious thoughts. See if there is any offensive way in me, and lead me in the way everlasting" (Psalm 139:23–24).

Discussion Questions

1. What is introspection?

2. List the dangers of introspection.

   The fascination with this subject matter is never a source of joy. It is a cause of depression.

3. What is the alternative to introspection (1 John 1:5–10 and James 1:17)?

   This is the message we have heard from him and declare to you; God is light and in him there is no darkness at all" (1 John 1:5).

4. How does the light that God provides differ from the light provided from introspection?

5. How does David look for sin in his life (Psalm 139:23–24)?

The Next Step: Responding to God's Word

Reflect on how you have dealt with past issues that have been done to you or that you have done and are ashamed of. Give these skeletons of sin to the Lord. Ask forgiveness, knowing it is immediate and complete because the blood of Jesus keeps on cleansing. Respond by walking in the light, allowing you to be all Christ has in mind for you. "Brothers, I do not consider myself yet to have taken hold of it. But one thing I do: Forgetting what is behind and straining toward what is ahead, I press on toward the goal to win the prize for which God has called me heavenward in Christ Jesus" (Phil. 3:13).

How to Receive Bitterness
(How to Handle Bitterness Against You)

Jim Wilson

Bless those who persecute you; bless and do not curse. (Rom. 12:14)

---

ow can we prevent others from being bitter toward us?

Now about food sacrificed to idols: We know that "We all possess knowledge." But knowledge puffs up while love builds up. Those who think they know something do not yet know as they ought to know. But whoever loves God is known by God. So then, about eating food sacrificed to idols: We know that "An idol is nothing at all in the world" and that "There is no God but one".... Be careful, however, that the exercise of your rights does not become a stumbling block to the weak. For if someone with a weak conscience sees you, with all your knowledge, eating in an idol's temple, won't that person be emboldened to eat what is sacrificed to idols? So this weak brother or sister, for whom Christ died, is destroyed by your knowledge. When you sin against them in this way and wound their weak conscience, you sin against Christ. Therefore, if what I eat causes my brother or sister to fall into sin, I will never eat meat again, so that I will not cause them to fall. (1 Cor. 8:1–4, 9–13)

"I have the right to do anything," you say—but not everything is beneficial. "I have the right to do anything"—but not everything is constructive. No one should seek their own good, but the good of others.... If an unbeliever invites you to a meal and you want to go, eat whatever is put before you without raising questions of conscience. But if someone says to you, "This has been offered in sacrifice," then do not eat it, both for the sake of the one who told you and for the sake of conscience. I am referring to the other person's conscience, not yours. For why is my freedom being judged by another's conscience? If I take part in the meal with thankfulness, why am I denounced because of something I thank God for? So whether you eat or drink or whatever you do, do it all for the glory of God. Do not cause anyone to stumble, whether Jews,

Greeks or the church of God—even as I try to please everyone in every way. For I am not seeking my own good but the good of many, so that they may be saved. (1 Cor. 10:23–24, 27–33)

Bless those who persecute you; bless and do not curse. Rejoice with those who rejoice; mourn with those who mourn. Live in harmony with one another. Do not be proud, but be willing to associate with people of low position. Do not be conceited. Do not repay anyone evil for evil. Be careful to do what is right in the eyes of everyone. If it is possible, as far as it depends on you, live at peace with everyone. Do not take revenge, my dear friends, but leave room for God's wrath, for it is written: "It is mine to avenge; I will repay," says the Lord. On the contrary: "If your enemy is hungry, feed him; if he is thirsty, give him something to drink. In doing this, you will heap burning coals on his head." Do not be overcome by evil, but overcome evil with good. (Rom. 12:14–21)

What if someone else is already bitter against you? Among your relatives, friends, and acquaintances, there are three types of people: those whom you are very close with, with no obstructions between you; those that you think have sinned against you; and those who think you have sinned against them. If someone is bitter towards you, it is probably someone close—a relative, friend (or former friend), or co-worker. What they hold against you may be something imaginary, a misunderstanding, or a sin you are really guilty of.

The Scripture has something to say about this: "Therefore, if you are offering your gift at the altar and there remember that your brother or sister has something against you, leave your gift there in front of the altar. First go and be reconciled to them; then come and offer your gift" (Matt. 5:23–24). We don't take gifts to the altar any more, but there are other things we do that are coming to the Lord. The most obvious is the Lord's Supper. You come to the Lord in this special remembrance, and 1 Corinthians 11 tells us to do it properly. "Properly" means that your heart must be clean. You come with your sins already forgiven, so you can observe it in real worship to God.

Three things stand out in this passage: 1) You know that your brother has something against you. 2) You need to be reconciled with your brother. 3) You are not to present your offering to God until reconciliation is accomplished.

How do you be reconciled? First, go to him. If you know what the problem is, and it is something you can fix by confessing to God and to your brother, do it. If you do not know what the problem is, ask him. If it is a legitimate charge, confess it to God and to him and ask for his forgiveness. If it is a misunderstanding or a rumor that is not true, explain it to him.

If the bitter person thinks that you owe him money, determine whether it is true. If it is, pay him the full amount plus 20 percent.

The Lord said to Moses: "If anyone sins and is unfaithful to the Lord by deceiving a neighbor about something entrusted to them or left in their care or about
something stolen, or if they cheat their neighbor, or if
they find lost property and lie about it, or if they swear
falsely about any such sin that people may commit—
when they sin in any of these ways and realize their
guilt, they must return what they have stolen or taken
by extortion, or what was entrusted to them, or the lost
property they found, or whatever it was they swore
falsely about. They must make restitution in full, add
a fifth of the value to it and give it all to the owner on
the day they present their guilt offering." (Lev. 6:1–5)

If you do not owe him the money, find out how much
he expects from you, double the amount, and give it
to him. "And if anyone wants to sue you and take your
shirt, hand over your coat as well" (Matt. 5:40).

If he has taken offense about something you said or
did that was not sin, do not apologize or say you are
sorry for it. That is a humanistic solution and will not
fix the problem. You would be apologizing for his taking offense. You would be apologizing for his sin. Giving
offence is sometimes sin. Taking offense is always sin.

If someone is bitter against you, go to him. You don't
have the option of not going. This is basic, groundwork
Christianity.

"But he won't listen."

How do you know he won't?

"My attitude's so bad, I'll fix it so he won't listen."

Spend time with the Lord before you go.

What about the opposite case, where someone has sinned against you? Matthew 18 addresses this. "If your brother sins, go and point out his fault, just between the two of you. If he listens to you, you have won him over" (Matt. 18:15). If he has something against you, go to him. If you have something against him, go to him. In both cases, you do the going.

When you go to be reconciled with your brother, how do you go? If he has sinned against you, you *may not* go to him with an accusatory attitude or accusatory words. The object of this process is reconciliation. When you go with an accusation, your object obviously is not reconciliation, and I can guarantee he won't listen to you.

The last verse of Matthew 18 says, "This is how my heavenly Father will treat each of you unless you forgive your brother or sister from your heart" (Matt. 18:35). That is right after the "seventy times seven" passage. It doesn't say to forgive him if he repents seventy times seven, but if he has *sinned* against you seventy times seven. Four hundred and ninety times you go to him with forgiveness in your heart. You bring his sin to attention, but your heart is forgiving. The object is to get him to repent, and you cannot do that with a belligerent attitude. You go to him for *his* sake. If he has sinned against you, he is in trouble.

Recently, I was talking to someone in this situation. I said, "If you did what you think this other person did, how would you feel?" (I find myself asking this question fairly often.)

He said, "I'd feel awful."

"Oh! So he must feel awful!" I asked him, "When do you hurt the most: when someone sins against you, or when you sin?"

"I hurt the most when I sin."

"This brother sinned against you. He must be hurting a lot. Go to him for his sake, not for your sake."

When you go with forgiveness, it turns out to be for both your sakes. Go with forgiveness in your *heart*, not in your mouth. If it's in your heart, it will get in your mouth, too, but you can put it in your mouth without it being real.

The times when people have come to me like this or I've gone to them, it has made all the difference in the world—we reconciled!

One of the basic teachings in Scripture is being eager to maintain the unity of the saints in the bond of peace. Some of the reconciling you do may be with non-Christian friends, but a lot of it is within the church of Jesus Christ. It may not be within the same church, but between two churches: in fact, that may be the reason they are two churches—because they split over attitudes. People are unwilling to tell the other person he is wrong kindly or admit that they are wrong kindly, humbly. And yet it is basic Christianity. If they have something against you, go to them. Reconciliation is primary.

If none of these things seems to work, then the bitter person is the one who needs the help. If he is still bitter after you go to him, someone else should minister to him. If you try to help him, he may just get more bitter. Do not get bitter in return. Do not lose your joy because your brother is in sin. Love him, pray for him, and take his accusations with joy.

> Blessed are you when people insult you, persecute you and falsely say all kinds of evil against you because of me. Rejoice and be glad, because great is your reward in heaven, for in the same way they persecuted the prophets who were before you. (Matt. 5:11–12)

> Bless those who persecute you; bless and do not curse. (Rom. 12:14)

> Do not repay anyone evil for evil. Be careful to do what is right in the eyes of everybody . . . . On the contrary: If your enemy is hungry, feed him; if he is thirsty, give him something to drink. In doing this, you will heap burning coals on his head. (Rom. 12:17, 20)

It is possible that the bitter person is not saved. In that case, he may not be able to forgive you or to get rid of his bitterness. What he needs is the Lord Jesus Christ. What should you do for his salvation?

• Live a godly life that cannot honestly be criticized.

- Love him in such a way that he knows that you love him.
- Follow the instructions in 2 Timothy 2:23–26: "Don't have anything to do with foolish and stupid arguments, because you know they produce quarrels. And the Lord's servant must not be quarrelsome but must be kind to everyone, able to teach, not resentful. Opponents must be gently instructed, in the hope that God will grant them repentance leading them to a knowledge of the truth, and that they will come to their senses and escape from the trap of the devil, who has taken them captive to do his will."
- Follow the instructions in Acts 26:15–18: "Then I asked, 'Who are you, Lord?' 'I am Jesus, whom you are persecuting,' the Lord replied. 'Now get up and stand on your feet. I have appeared to you to appoint you as a servant and as a witness of what you have seen and will see of me. I will rescue you from your own people and from the Gentiles. I am sending you to them to open their eyes and turn them from darkness to light, and from the power of Satan to God, so that they may receive forgiveness of sins and a place among those who are sanctified by faith in me.'"

If you follow these instructions, you will no longer be the person that he is bitter towards. You will have become his spiritual parent.

Study Guide

Bless those who persecute you: bless and do not curse. (Rom. 12-14)

Discussion Questions

1. Do you have someone in your life that is bitter against you? If so, what steps have you taken to restore this relationship?

2. Why is it important to address bitterness against you as soon as possible (Matt. 5:23-24 and Heb. 12:14)?

3. Matthew 18:15-19 provides a biblical model for addressing bitterness and restoring a relationship between believers. How can you apply Jesus' instructions for reconciliation in your life?

4. Restoring a relationship requires seeking God's wisdom in prayer, humility, and a sincere desire to reconcile. As believers in Christ, how should we address grievances against each other (Col. 3:13)?

5. Why does the Bible teach us to "bless those who persecute you" even if the bitter person refuses to listen (Rom. 12:14-21, Eph. 4:31-5:2)?

The Next Step: Responding to God's Word

Reflect on a relationship that you know needs to be restored. Ask God for wisdom, strength, and courage as you seek to reconcile this relationship. Respond in love as God provides opportunities for healing. "Make every effort to keep the unity of the Spirit through the bond of peace" (Eph. 4:3).

Relationships with Parents

Jim Wilson

Honor your father and your mother, so that you may live long in the land the Lord your God is giving you. (Exod. 20:12)

O f the many talks I frequently give, those which have received the most favorable response and the most fruitful application among young and old alike are "How to Be Free from Bitterness" and "Relationships with Parents." Right now, I am sitting in a study room at the Illinois Street Residence Hall at the University of Illinois. Last week, at Urbana '93, I conducted a workshop on relationships with parents. Only about 50 students attended the workshop. The shock, the incredulity, the rebellion, and the impossibility of putting this teaching into effect showed in the tears, the questions, the comments, and the follow-up conversations. That is why I am here writing it down.

I would first like to draw your attention to two passages in the Old Testament. I will comment on them, then make a few suggestions for applying these Scriptures in your life.

> You shall not make for yourself an idol in the form of anything in heaven above or on the earth beneath or in the waters below. You shall not bow down to them or worship them; for I, the Lord your God, am a jealous God, punishing the children for the sin of the fathers to the third and fourth generation of those who hate me, but showing love to thousands who love me and keep my commandments. (Deut. 5:8–10)

> Yet you ask, "Why does the son not share the guilt of his father?" Since the son has done what is just and right and has been careful to keep all my decrees, he will surely live. The soul who sins is the one who will die. The son will not share the guilt of the father, nor will the father share the guilt of the son. The righteousness of the righteous man will be credited to him, and the wickedness of the wicked will be charged against him. (Ezek. 18:19–20)

When we read in Deuteronomy 5:10, "punishing the children for the sin of the fathers to the third and fourth generation of those who hate me," we could conclude that this is not just. However, throughout the entire eighteenth chapter of Ezekiel, we see that children are not held responsible for the sins of their fathers. So what is the second commandment saying? It is saying that sin flows downhill. The sinful influence of our ancestors affects us, overlapping and passing through several generations. This is generational bad news.

However, the sentence does not end with verse 9; it continues with "but showing love to thousands who love me and keep my commandments." The word "thousands" is really "thousands of generations," in contrast to three or four generations. How do we know it is "thousands of generations"? First, it is the only way the sentence makes sense, and, second, two chapters later we have an explicit statement to that effect: "Know therefore that the Lord your God is God; he is the faithful God, keeping his covenant of love to a thousand generations of those who love him and keep his commands" (Deut. 7:9). Sin and hatred of God cause the downward movement to three or four generations, and obedience and love of God cause the upward movement to a thousand generations.

I have heard this many times: "I decided I was not going to be the kind of father (or mother) who raised me. I would become a Christian, marry a Christian, and do it right. I became a Christian, married a Christian, and I am doing it wrong, just like my parents. I am in the second bad-news generation; do I have to wait for two more bad generations before it is possible to turn this descent around?"

No, you do not have to wait, but unless you change your relationship with your parents and grandparents you will have to wait two more generations. Becoming a Christian and preaching the gospel to your parents does not change the relationship. Home, with parents, is one of the places where Christians think that they are allowed to lose their temper. That makes the relationship get worse.

About 400 years before Christ, the prophet Malachi gave a negative conditional prophecy. It is found in the last two verses in the Old Testament. "See, I will send you the prophet Elijah before the great and dreadful day of the Lord comes. He will turn the hearts of the fathers to their children, and the hearts of the children to their fathers; or else I will come and strike the land with a curse" (Mal. 4:5–6).

The angel Gabriel alludes to this prophecy in Luke 1:17: "And he [John] will go on before the Lord, in the spirit and power of Elijah, to turn the hearts of the fathers to their children and the disobedient to the wisdom of the righteous, to make ready a people prepared for the Lord."

Notice that to stop the curse from happening, hearts must be turned both ways. Although most of my illustrations are speaking to and about children, I am really speaking to parents about their relationship with their own parents. If you are a Christian parent, turn your heart toward your parents, and turn your heart toward your children.

Now look at the second instance where the Ten Commandments speak of generations. "Honor your father and mother, as the Lord your God has commanded you, so that you may live long and that it may go well with you in the land the Lord your God is giving you" (Deut. 5:16).

Application is next: love God (Deut. 5:9); obey God (Deut. 5:9); honor your father and mother (Deut. 5:16); and turn your hearts to your fathers (Mal. 4:5–6).

Because we have not obeyed the two passages in the Ten Commandments, we may be in the third- and fourth-generation promise, and we will not live long on the earth (cf. Eph. 6:1). The land is in danger of being smitten with a curse. The Malachi text is a call to repentance, a turnaround of the heart.

Here are a few suggestions on how to have a heart repentance that will 1) stop the curse, 2) cause long life, and 3) turn the three or four generations of bad news around to a thousand generations of good news.

First, there are a few things that are very important in this turnaround, though they alone bring no automatic guarantee of halting the curse.

1. Become a Christian. Without a conversion to Christ, it is impossible to love and obey God.

2. Marry a Christian. Without a Christian marriage, you have no assurance that you will have Christian children.

3. Stay married. "To the married I give this command . . . . A wife must not separate from her

husband . . . and a husband must not divorce his wife" (1 Cor. 7:10–11).

Without these three, you can expect more bad generations. However, with them, the bad generations may still happen. Why? Because your prior generations still affect you and your children. Leaving your father and mother and cleaving to your wife does not mean that you have turned your heart to your father. Until you do, you are asking for another generation of bad news. You cannot expect to be a good husband or a good father if you have not turned your heart to your own father.

In turning your heart to your father, four elements are necessary. Preaching the gospel to him is not one of them; do not do so, for this subverts his authority over you. Instead, you may write a letter him that conveys each of these four elements. I recommend covering one element per paragraph as follows:

1. If you have confessed to God your previous rebellion to your father or mother, also confess it to your earthly father with no excuses or accusations.

2. Tell your father how much you respect him. If you do not respect him, of course you cannot write it without being hypocritical. But you must write it. How?

    First confess to God this disrespect for your father. "Why should I? He has not earned it!" The

Scripture says, "Honor your father and mother." It does not say "only if they deserve it." Your father is to be honored because he is your father. You are commanded to honor him. This is not optional. If you do not honor him, then you have sinned. The same is true with your mother. Sin is forgivable, and repentance is required.

After you have confessed your disrespect or lack of honor for your father, and you are sure you are forgiven, choose to respect him. You may ask, "How? He is not respectable." Respect has nothing to do with the respectableness of the person to be respected. It has to do with the respecter and the respecter's close fellowship with and obedience to God.

Now with freedom and sincerity, write to your father how much you respect him in this second paragraph.

3. In the third paragraph, tell him how much you love him. If you do not love him, that has to be corrected first. Your reply may be, "He did not love me, so I do not love him." It is true that, as a father, he should have loved you so that your response would have been a loving response. But we cannot go back to childhood and start over. Even if we could, that does not guarantee that your father would do it any different the second time. We address the problem from where we are, not from where we should be. You are now an adult, and as a Christian you have

unlimited access to love and forgiveness. If you do not have this access, there is a very real possibility that you are not a Christian. As a Christian, you may have to confess this lack of love for your father to God. Is it sin? Yes, it is sin. It is disobedience to the command of God. We have been commanded to love our neighbors, love the brothers, and love our enemies. If you do not think your father fits in one of these categories, then perhaps you should study the unconditional quality of love and the biblical relationship of obedience and love.

After you have confessed and have been forgiven, choose to love your father. This love requires expression, so tell him in this paragraph.

4. The next paragraph is the place to express your gratefulness to him. If you are not grateful, then as with respect and love, it is your problem, not his. The procedure is the same. Confess your unthankfulness to God. When you are forgiven, express your thankfulness to your father.

These four elements are necessary and required. The next two are suggestions for further ways to convey respect.

5. Ask your father to tell you or write you his autobiography, his life history. He might not do it, but he will be glad you want to know about him.

6. Ask him for advice and counsel, in general and on specific matters. This is part of honor.

Write the same kind of letter to your mother, but with one change. The first paragraph should express your love to her, and the second paragraph should communicate your respect for her. Both sexes of the human race need love and respect from both sexes. Of the two, women need love more than they need respect, and men need respect more than they need love. However, each needs both, and they should not have to earn it in order to receive it.

This letter should be followed up with other kind personal letters, hugs, and other physical expressions (e.g. handshakes, if they are warm, firm, and exuberant).

The letter can be followed up with an explanation, as long as the explanation does not include excuses or accusations. Here is a suggestion: "Dad, I know that you love me very much. You have not been the best expresser of your love. So growing up I did not think you loved me. Even now I have had to take it by faith. If you wondered why I was boy crazy from junior high through college, it was because I was looking for male affection. Of course, I did not get it. I was getting taken. Now you are wondering about my letter to you and all of the hugs you are getting from me when I come to visit. Although I now have a husband and children, I still need my father, and you need me. That's why I am here hugging you. I thought I would prime the pump. I'm giving to receive." Adjust this example to fit you.

When your parents receive these two letters, several things will probably happen. The letter will be read more than once, it will not be thrown away, and you will receive some sort of favorable response. If you do not receive a response, do not think that you did something wrong. Be patient and keep on giving. Some cultures (e.g. those of Northern Europe) are not expressive with their emotions, except for lost tempers. This kind of expression from you may be embarrassing for your parents. But they still want to receive this expressed love even if they do not know how to return it.

One man in his late fifties wrote this kind of letter to his father. His mother replied. "I have been married to your father for sixty years. When he read your letter, that was the first time in our marriage I saw tears in his eyes."

In the early 1980s, we held a summer school of practical Christianity at Delta House of the University of Idaho. About 40 students attended. Respect for parents was one of the subjects. The following fall, in a noon Bible class at Washington State University, I was teaching on the same subject again. One of the students spoke up. He gave us a story that went something like this:

"I learned this last summer at the Delta House. When I was sixteen, my father kicked me out of the house, saying that he would never see me again. I left home. I later became a Christian and married a Christian. Now I am a graduate student in economics at WSU. In the meantime, I had not seen my father. My parents were on the brink of divorce, living in separate bedrooms at home (in one of the Great Plains states).

"When I learned this material, I wrote two letters, one to my father and one to my mother. It took me several days to write each one, so they were sent several days apart. For some reason, the letters arrived on the same day, and both my parents were at home. Seeing that the letters were addressed separately, my mother took her letter to her room, and my father took his letter to his room. After reading the letters, they exchanged them and went again to their separate rooms and read. When they came out, my father had tears in his eyes and said, 'I'm flying out to Pullman to see my son.' I have seen my father since last summer, and my parents' marriage has been saved."

There are two problems, the heart problem and the action problem. The heart problem is first. Your unlove, your disrespect, your ungratefulness have to be taken care of in repentance toward God. To write a letter without being forgiven by God only ensures that your letter will be insincere and hypocritical.

You may have a long wait if you wait for your father to turn to you first. You cannot afford the wait.

After you are clean, write the letters. Then continue letter-writing, telephoning, and visiting, expressing respect, love, and thankfulness.

Doing these things will change you. You will become a better husband, son, and father, or a better wife, daughter, and mother. Your love and obedience will bring love for a thousand generations.

Study Guide

You shall not make for yourself an idol in the form of anything in heaven above or on the earth beneath or in the waters below. You shall not bow down to them or worship them; for I, the Lord your God, am a jealous God, punishing the children for the sin of the fathers to the third and fourth generation of those who hate me, but showing love to thousands who love me and keep my commandments. (Deut. 5:8–10)

Discussion Questions

1. What does Deuteronomy 5:8–10 tell us about the sins of our ancestors?

2. What does God promise to those who love Him and keep His commandments (Deut. 5:10)?

3. What needs to take place to stop the sins of the father from being passed on from one generation to the next (Mal. 4:5–6 and Luke 1:17)?

   Honor your father and mother, as the Lord your God has commanded you, so that you may live long and that it may go well with you in the land the Lord your God is giving you. (Deut. 5:16)

4. What enables us to turn our hearts towards our father or mother (Deut. 5:9, 16 and Malachi 4:5–6)?

5. What steps can be taken towards developing a heart of repentance and turning the three or four generations of bad news to a thousand generations of good news?

The Next Step: Responding to God's Word
Reflect on bitterness and anger that you have been unable to let go of on your own. Ask God to enable you to give up the bitterness, give up the anger, and give up the feelings of injustice to Him. Respond through confession, allowing your heart to be cleansed and renewed. Then consider writing a letter using the four elements listed. "Know therefore that the Lord your God is God; he is the faithful God, keeping his covenant of love to a thousand generations of those who love him and keep his commands" (Deut. 7:9).

Saturation Love

Jim Wilson

Give, and it will be given to you. A good measure, pressed down, shaken together and running over, will be poured into your lap. For with the measure you use, it will be measured to you. (Luke 6:38)

G od gives commands to love. These commands are to be applied to wives, brothers, neighbors, aliens, and enemies. This love is the love that God had for us when Jesus Christ died for us. It is sacrificial; its primary expression is giving. It is designed to be effective. It worked for our salvation.

Love requires an object, and love requires expression. "For God so loved the world that he gave . . . "

(John 3:16). The world was love's object, and giving was love's expression. This love was not half-hearted or reluctant or "almost enough." It was complete and more than adequate for all of the sins and sinners in this world. "But where sin increased, grace increased all the more . . ." (Romans 5:20).

In obeying God's commands to love, we are to love as He loved. That is unconditional and without reserve or reluctance. We should have and give more love to the person needing love so that his need for love is satisfied. You may think that that is impossible. This person is so starved for love that loving him is like pouring water down a rat hole. You are convinced that you will run out of love before this love-starved person is satiated. That might be true if you are counting on him returning love to meet your needs. But if you get refilled by the Holy Spirit, you are never going to run out.

Now let's apply this principle to raising children. There are many different problems in raising children that require understanding and applying biblical principles. Here are a few of these problems:

- Lack of obedience
- Lack of effective discipline for disobedience
- Lack of effective training and teaching
- Sibling rivalry and jealousy
- Attention-getting devices such as whining, crying, and tantrums

- Signs of insecurity such as speaking loudly, warts, overweight, scratching, hitting, biting, picking at the body, and hand mannerisms

Each of these subjects could fill a book; in fact, books have been written on each of them. You may have read some of them and implemented what you learned, and, with some of you, what you applied did not work. It is easy to draw the conclusion that the book was wrong. The book may have been right, and your application may have been right. What went wrong?

Here is the principle mentioned earlier. I will call it saturation love. Saturation love is different from adequate love, quality time, or quantity time. It includes the last two plus undivided attention.

Saturation means that maximum absorption has been reached. A saturated solution is one where the solvent cannot dissolve anymore solute. For example, if you continue to add and stir sugar into a glass of water, the water will eventually become saturated with sugar, meaning no more sugar will dissolve in it. After the solution reaches the saturation point, any additional sugar will fall to the bottom of the glass—the water cannot dissolve anymore.

It is the same with love. It is possible to saturate someone with love so that any additional love is not received. It is not rejected; it is just not needed.

Over the years, I asked audiences for a show of hands if they thought their parents loved them. Over 95% of the hands would go up. It was never 100%, but it was always a high percentage. Then I asked this question of those who had raised their hands: "Do you think that your parents expressed this love to you adequately?" Only half of the hands stayed up. The third question was, "Of those of you who think your parents expressed their love for you adequately, could you have used an even greater expression of love?" All of the hands remained up.

- No love
- Some love
- Adequate love
- Even more love is wanted.

No one ever thought he received enough love from his parents. Their children will, if asked, say the same thing about them.

What are the consequences of not getting enough love? Disobedience is directly proportional to the shortfall in love.[3] Even if administered correctly, discipline for the disobedience is not effective if the child is not loved enough. He thinks, "The last time I got any attention around here was the last time I got spanked." Disobedience becomes his means for getting attention. Therefore, your training and teaching is ineffective if you are not giving your child enough love.

3 We know that the child is born with, and later practices, a sinful nature. This sinful nature is the primary reason for his disobedience, and that changes at his conversion. Both before and after conversion, his disobedience is affected by lack of love.

The amount of sibling rivalry, competition, self-ishness, and jealousy is inversely proportional to the love shown to your children. When all of the kids are saturated with love, there will be little or no rivalry, squabbles, or fights. The more love, the less whining, disobedience, and jealousy, and the less crying and tantrums. Also, the more love, the sooner the child will become a Christian.

"Or do you show contempt for the riches of his kindness, tolerance and patience, not realizing that God's kindness leads you toward repentance?" (Rom. 2:14). God's means of leading us to repentance was to pour on the kindness and show us tolerance and patience even when we were sinners. How much more should we do this for our children!

What are our problems? We do not want to give hugs and attention to a whiner. We do not want to endorse bad behavior. That is true, but doing this is not endorsing bad behavior. It is curing it. This giving is not giving in to the child's dictations, but to his real need. His perception is more true than your perception. The "whiner" is asking for attention—loving attention. We will give a small baby attention when it cries. There may be nothing wrong; he is not hungry, wet, dirty, or sick; he just wants some loving. When the child is two or three or nine or ten and asks for attention, we do not want to give it. We do not think the child needs it. Believe me, if he asks for it, he needs it. When he is saturated, he will quit asking. (On the other hand, there are some children who need attention but will not demand it. They need and receive even less than the demander. Because they are not demanding, you may think they are satisfied.)

Our problem is that we run out of "give" before the child runs out of demand. We think he will never quit demanding our attention, so we quit giving it before we should quit. If we kept on giving the attention, we would find our child would get satisfied. The child will get full, and consequently he will be very secure and ask for very little in the years to come. This security is of central importance in your child's obedience to you.

Many years ago, there was a little boy who had warts on his left hand and arm. I think there were eighteen of them. He had had them for many months.

One day his father asked him, "Johnny would you like me to pray to God to take away your warts?"

Johnny replied, "No, they are my friends; I play with them."

His father knew that these warts were evidence of the boy's insecurity and that the insecurity was the result of the father himself not giving his son enough loving attention. The father made a decision and followed through with much loving attention. The warts disappeared in a very short time.

Many years ago, I was close to a young family who had four preschool boys ages one, two, three, and four. One day the parents came to see me about their oldest son. He had two major problems that they did not seem able to correct. 1) He was hitting each of his little brothers all day long. He was corrected on each occurrence, either shouted at, spanked, or both. 2) He had picked the skin off of his face in many places so that he had small red scabs all over his face. He looked like he had the measles.

The spankings did not seem to work. Their question was obvious: "What do we do?"

My answer was as follows: "The next time he hits a little brother, pick him up and hug him."

The mother answered, "I don't want to reinforce that kind of conduct."

"Don't worry. He already has gotten the message that it is wrong. Not only should you hug him the next time he hits his brother, I want you to hug him all day long. He hasn't gotten enough love since the second son was born, and now there are numbers three and four. The only time he gets attention is when he is bad. So he hits little brothers in order to get attention. He picks his face because he is insecure. I guarantee that if you pour loving attention on him with overkill, his face will clear up, and he will quit hitting his little brothers within two weeks."

She said, "I don't think I can do that."

"Why not?"

"I don't even like him anymore."

The parents confessed their sin and put this into effect. The predicted results came true.

Another time, a father with a very active 12-year-old son came to me for help. The son had had extensive discipline for misbehaving on small things and did not seem to have learned from the discipline. He also had a difficult time getting along with his peers. The parents were giving him a fair amount of love, attention, and time, but he still would not receive correction or be repentant when spanked repeatedly.

I told the father that he could not pour on too much love. In desperation to see improvement, the father poured on the physical affection and reduced the constant verbal correction of minor things. The father then took the boy to a men's retreat where he held the son in his arms for the two-hour van ride there and back, plus holding the son during the speaking sessions. Upon their return home, the mother immediately recognized a change in the boy's attitude and his willingness to receive correction without pouting, as well as his desire to get along better with other children.

In years of asking questions and listening to answers, there is one answer that stands out. "I never heard my father admit that he was wrong about anything. In the meantime, Mom knew he was wrong; we kids knew he was wrong; God knew he was wrong, and he himself knew it, but he would not admit it." This may be true of some of you fathers whose children are grown and gone. You may be reading this and realize that you did not practice saturation love when they were growing up. In the meantime, they have had all kinds of problems. Others of you have children who are teenagers, not away from home, but not little "lovable" kids.

What can you do about it now? First confess to God all of your wrong actions such as over-discipline, put-downs, ridicule, ignoring, yelling, anger, favoritism, lack of expressed love, etc. After this, you can write to each of your children expressing to them what you have confessed to God. Tell them you have confessed your actions and attitudes to God. You can also admit specific things that you remember. Ask the children to bring to your attention things that they are still hurting about, just as you may still be hurting about how your father treated you. When they tell you, do not be defensive; just be sorry with a godly sorrow. "Godly sorrow brings repentance that leads to salvation and leaves no regret, but worldly sorrow brings death" (2 Cor. 7:10). Then express love to them in many ways. If your children are still with you, do the same, except it should be in person in addition to the letter. The letter is important because 1) you can get it all said without interruptions, 2) the letter will get read many times, and 3) the letter will be kept.

Remember, both sexes of children need much love from both sexes of parents. If you are divorced, saturation love is more difficult, but still necessary. If you are competing for the love and loyalty of your children by putting down your former spouse or by buying your children's love, it is counterproductive. Not only is it less than saturation love, it is not love at all.

One of the best ways to express love to your children is by not fighting with your spouse. Fights between the parents is a major cause of insecurity in children. If you do disagree, the children should never hear it. If you already have a history of fighting or disagreeing with your spouse in front of the children, confess your history to God, then to your spouse and your children, and then forsake the fighting.

Study Guide

For God loved the world so much that he gave his only Son so that anyone who believes in him shall not perish but have eternal life. (John 3:16)

Discussion Questions

1. List reasons why a person may feel starved for love.

   Saturation love is different from adequate love, quality time, or quantity time. Saturation means that the maximum has been reached: a person's need to be loved has been completely filled.

2. Describe a situation where you received saturation love or were able to provide saturation love for another person.

3. What are the symptoms of not getting enough love?

   God leads us to repentance by pouring on kindness, showing us tolerance and patience even though we sin against Him. This is the model that God has put before us as parents.

4. How can God's model be applied when we parent our children?

5. What steps can we take to right the wrongs we have committed?

The Next Step: Responding to God's Word

Sins that are not confessed hold us back from a closer relationship with God and others in our life. We must confess our sin to God and ask Him to help us correct the sin. God asks us to respond by confessing our sin to our spouse and our children with a kind, compassionate, and tender heart. "Be kind and compassionate to one another, forgiving each other, just as in Christ God forgave you" (Eph. 4:32).

How Does a Woman Become Secure?

Jim Wilson

And my God will meet all your needs according to His glorious riches in Christ Jesus. (Phil. 4:19)

Awoman was made by God to be loved, protected, provided for, and made secure. However, there are reasons a woman may not feel loved, protected, or secure. Security is often a combination of objective truth and subjective feeling. What I mean by that is that some women have lost their parents, their husbands, their children, their food, and their clothing. Objectively they have a reason to be insecure, but subjectively they might not feel insecure. At the same time, it is possible to feel insecure and imagine what is objectively necessary to fill this need.

Here is an example: Suppose a woman feels insecure. The feeling is so strong that she is convinced that it is also objective truth. A woman's great need is to fill up that emptiness. She thinks that a man will fill it. That is partly true. However, the need is so great that the man she gets cannot fill it. He cannot because he is also empty and is looking for a woman to fill his emptiness. Two empty, insecure people marry each other to get their own needs met. It does not work.

Now the woman is even more insecure. She thinks that if she has a baby that will meet her need. Again, that is partly true. Women were made to have babies. However, babies are needy, demanding creatures. The insecure woman now has greater demands on her than she is able to cope with, especially if there are multiple children.

Now she is insecure and frazzled. She thinks she needs a nicer home with nicer furniture. That takes a lot of money. She has to work as well as her husband.

Now she is tired, insecure, and frazzled. She turns to clothes, music, parties, and maybe a different man. Her husband is not romantic. He copped out early in the marriage because his needs were not being met.

This is a description of many women I am acquainted with. Some of them have been married more than once, plus other men. Some of them are into possessions. They are finding out, rather late, that a man, children, house, possessions, and parties do not fill up their emptiness and give them the security they are looking for.

This need has to be met, but the selfishness that insists on it being met ensures that it will not be met even if she gets the man, the children, the house, and possessions. The selfishness has to go first. It has become a tight little fist in her soul. That selfish, tight fist wizens and destroys the person with it.

Before God, the selfishness has to be repented of, that is, confessed, forsaken, and renounced. Then she will have a wonderful joy, peace, and freedom which God will give to her. This will make her very secure in Christ.

As far as security in this world, the provision comes from a closeness to her father, mother, brothers, sisters, and extended family. Next, it comes from her brothers and sisters in Christ who are loving and giving. It comes from her being loving and giving to all kinds of people, even if they do not return the love. It could come from her husband, but not from a future husband. I say this because she should not get married in order to get secure. She should be secure before she gets married. Then she will not be disillusioned and hurt in her marriage.

How does a woman become secure?

She must confess her attitude, not just her action. She must decide, with the grace of God, to love her father, mother, brothers, and sisters. Her love towards any of them cannot be conditional. She should not say, "I will love him if . . . " No "ifs." This love includes kind speech, hugs, giving, and helping actions. She should extend this love to more and more people. "For Christ's love compels us, because we are convinced that one died for all, and therefore all died. And he died for all, that those who live should no longer live for themselves but for him who died for them and was raised again" (2 Cor. 5:14–15).

A woman's long-term objective should be to be holy, loving, kind, joyful, etc. She should also want to have a loving family and loving children and grandchildren. She should want to have a "Well done, good and faithful servant, enter into the joy of the Lord."

This solution assumes that the woman is already a Christian, that she has by faith received Jesus Christ, the Son of God, as Lord and Savior. She has passed from death to life. That is the beginning of security for everyone, men and women.

Study Guide

And my God will meet all your needs according to His glorious riches in Christ Jesus. (Phil. 4:19)

Discussion Questions

1. What does the Bible say about feeling safe and secure in the following verses?

Deuteronomy 33:12
Psalm 4:8
Proverbs 29:25
1 John 5:18

2. What does the Bible have to say about being satisfied?

Proverbs 30:15-16
Ecclesiastes 5:10
Psalm 63:5
Psalm 103:5
Isaiah 53:11

Do nothing out of selfish ambition or vain conceit, but in humility consider others better than yourselves. (Phil. 2:3)

3. How can we rid ourselves of selfishness?

4. What steps need to be taken to feel secure (James 3:13-18)?

The Next Step: Responding to God's Word
Reflect on areas in your life where bitter envy and selfish ambition hinder your ability to be an imitator of Christ. Ask for godly wisdom and discernment to guide you. Respond by seeking His direction each day. "Ask and it will be given to you; seek and you will find; knock and the door will be opened to you. For everyone

who asks receives; he who seeks finds; and to him who knocks, the door will be opened" (Matt. 7:7–8).

The Responsible Man

Jim Wilson

Be on your guard; stand firm in the faith; be men of courage; be strong. (1 Cor. 16:13)

*I*f there is one great lack in adult men, Christian and non-Christian, it is integrity. That is a word that encompasses honesty, moral soundness, purity, uprightness, and the willingness to take responsibility. It is this last aspect of integrity that I would like to address.

Responsibility is one of the characteristics of a selfless man. Irresponsibility is one of the characteristics of a selfish man. After a person receives Christ, responsibility should be an expected characteristic.

God has assigned responsibilities to kings, governors, masters, husbands, and fathers. God holds us responsible, whether or not we are acting responsibly. If we do not fit any of the above positions, we should be in training to be responsible. It is part of manhood.

We tend to have a worldly view of manliness, i.e., that it is determined by testosterone and its results: fighting, drinking too much, playing football, hunting, soldiering, sexual prowess, and authority. In many cases, putting an emphasis on these characteristics actually keeps a man from accepting responsibility, which is his real evidence of manhood.

Adam was irresponsible when he said to God in Genesis 3:12, "The woman you put here with me—she gave me some fruit from the tree, and I ate." Adam blamed the woman and God. God replied in Genesis 3:17. "To Adam he said, 'Because you listened to your wife and ate from the tree about which I commanded you, "You must not eat of it," cursed is the ground because of you; through painful toil you will eat of it all the days of your life.'"

Ever since that time, men have been blaming their wives, their children, and their bosses, and everyone but themselves.

Abram was also irresponsible: "As he was about to enter Egypt, he said to his wife Sarai, 'I know what a beautiful woman you are. When the Egyptians see you, they will say, "This is his wife." Then they will kill me but will let you live. Say you are my sister, so that

I will be treated well for your sake and my life will be spared because of you'" (Gen. 12:11–13). Abram anticipated being killed by the Egyptians for his beautiful wife. He had her tell a lie and say she was not his wife, but his sister. Pharaoh took her and treated Abram well and made him rich. God afflicted Pharaoh and his household with serious disease because he had taken Abram's wife to be his wife. When Pharaoh found out, he gave Sarai back and kicked Abram out of the country.

About twenty years later, Abram, now called Abraham, did the same thing again with another king of another nation, only that time he lied instead of having Sarah lie. Abimelech, the king of Gerar, took her. God told Abimelech that he was as good as dead for taking a married woman. God protected Sarah. Abimelech had not touched her. You can read the story in Genesis 20.

This irresponsibility was passed on to Isaac. He lied to the same king about Rebekah. The unbelievers had a greater conscience about this than Abraham and Isaac. They had scorn for the irresponsibility of the believers (Gen. 26). Sarah and Rebekah were weaker and innocent.

Irresponsibility is a special kind of sin. It is a sin that holds other people responsible. Irresponsibility is like lying. It is a cover, a means of self-protection. It is selfishness to the extreme. We see it in disclaiming fatherhood, not paying child support, blaming others, wife-beating, verbal abuse, not providing, and not giving love and protection.

Here are a few examples of responsible men in the Bible: the official in John 4:46–53, Cornelius in Acts 10, the jailer at Philippi in Acts 16, and the apostle Paul in 1 Corinthians 9 and 2 Corinthians 8.

Additional teaching on responsibility can be found in Numbers 30:6–8. This is in relation to the women in your home, your wife and your daughters.

There are two things that cannot be separated without causing much harm to those around you. They are authority and responsibility.

Consider little kids. One of the kids wants authority. He wants to be boss. When there is trouble as the result of his leadership, he is not to be found, or he blames the trouble on the other kids. He does not want the responsibility that comes with his authority.

We have seen this problem in kings throughout history, and in the recent presidents of the United States. When they were president, they had more authority than anyone else in the world.

President Truman used his authority. He also accepted the responsibility for his actions. He kept a sign on his desk which read, "The buck stops here." He would not pass the buck. President Clinton and President Obama also used their authority, but they did not hesitate to be evasive, lie, and blame others. In integrity, they were not responsible husbands, fathers, governors/senators, or presidents.

As a husband, a father, a pastor or a leader in a secular job, a Christian man does not have the privilege of being a boss. Even in his position of leadership, he is commanded by God.

- As a husband: "Husbands, love your wives, just as Christ loved the church and gave himself up for her to make her holy, cleansing her by the washing with water through the word, and to present her to himself as a radiant church, without stain or wrinkle or any other blemish, but holy and blameless. In this same way, husbands ought to love their wives as their own bodies. He who loves his wife loves himself. After all, no one ever hated his own body, but he feeds and cares for it, just as Christ does the church—for we are members of his body" (Eph. 5:25–30).

- As a father: "Fathers, do not exasperate your children; instead, bring them up in the training and instruction of the Lord" (Eph. 6:4).

- As a master: "And masters, treat your slaves in the same way. Do not threaten them, since you know that he who is both their Master and yours is in heaven, and there is no favoritism with him" (Eph. 6:9).

- As an elder: "To the elders among you, I appeal as a fellow elder, a witness of Christ's sufferings and one who also will share in the glory to be revealed: Be shepherds of God's flock that is

under your care, serving as overseers—not because you must, but because you are willing,
as God wants you to be; not greedy for money,
but eager to serve; not lording it over those entrusted to you, but being examples to the flock.
And when the Chief Shepherd appears, you will
receive the crown of glory that will never fade
away" (1 Pet. 5:1–4).

Notice the absence of instruction to be dictatorial
over your subordinates. Notice the positive attitudes
and actions required of the husband, father, master,
and elder. Part of our responsibility is to train our sons
to be responsible.

How do you get to be a responsible man?

- Recognize the attributes of a responsible
  Christian man.
- Confess the sins of your negative attitude and
  actions.
- Choose to be obedient to God's commands in
  the Bible.
- Attach yourself to a responsible man you can
  imitate.
- Choose to be taught by responsible men person-
  ally or through books, blogs, talks, podcasts, etc.

If you are not a Christian, seek out a Christian and
tell him you want to become one. Read the gospel

article at the end of this booklet. Get a Bible and read Luke, John, Acts, and Romans.

If you are a Christian, you need to:

- Confess your sin and sins to God. Be specific with the confession. Let's make it stronger: confess and forsake them. Renounce them. Repudiate them! Repent of them to God and receive the cleansing and purifying work of the blood of Christ (1 John 1:5–10).
- Be obedient. By the grace of God, refuse to blame others for something that happened when you were in charge.
- Choose to supply spiritual leadership, food, housing, love, security, protection, and comfort for your wife and children. That is your number-one job.
- After you have confessed, get with a man who is willing to teach you, by example and instruction, how to be responsible.
- Be in the Book daily, reading and studying with the intention of obeying God.
- Ask for God's help.

Study Guide

For we are each responsible for our own conduct. (Gal. 6:5)

Discussion Questions

1. A person of integrity can be defined as one who does the right thing even when no one is looking. Who is a person of integrity in your life? What character qualities do you admire most in this person?

   Integrity encompasses honesty, moral soundness, purity, uprightness, and the willingness to take responsibility.

2. 1 Corinthians 16:13 reminds us to "Be on your guard; stand firm in the faith; be men of courage; be strong." What steps can you take to stand firm in your faith and guard your heart from selfish desires (Prov. 3:5-6, Matt. 22:37-39, and Phil. 4:4-13)?

3. God has given us the gift of the Holy Spirit to guide our hearts. How does the Holy Spirit help you in times of weakness (Rom. 8:26-28)?

4. A responsible Christian man reflects the character of Christ (Gal. 5:22-23) in all situations. He gives up his selfish desires so that the Holy Spirit can produce spiritual fruit that brings God glory and blesses his future generations. What situations,

attitudes, or actions are standing in the way of you becoming a responsible man in Christ?

5. The Apostle Paul encourages us to "put off" our old way of life from before we believed in Christ and "put on" a new self, allowing the Holy Spirit to work in us and guide us (Gal. 5:16-26 and Eph. 4:22-5:2). How has your relationship with Jesus Christ changed the way you live, love, and serve others?

The Next Step: Responding to God's Word

Do you know a person of integrity and faith that can help you grow in grace and the knowledge of the Lord Jesus Christ? If not, ask God to help you find a mentor or small group to meet with on a regular basis. Confess areas in your life where you are struggling with responsibility and integrity. Trust God to provide the courage and strength needed to stand firm in your faith. Respond by listening to the Holy Spirit's guidance and obeying God's Word. "Your ears will hear a voice behind you saying, This is the way; walk in it" (Isa. 30:21).

Questions & Answers on Becoming a Christian

Jim Wilson

For the wages of sin is death, but the gift of God is eternal life in Christ Jesus our Lord. (Rom. 6:23)

Sometime in 1997, a woman picked up a free copy of *How to Be Free from Bitterness*. She was shaken by reading it and sent me a postcard. I realized that she was hurting badly, so I telephoned her to see if I could help. She wrote to me again. I kept her letters and copies of my answers. The following is three months of our correspondence. With her permission, we made copies to help people with similar questions and wound up handing out thousands of them. We have included the correspondence here, and we hope it will be a help to some of you who have had a similar background.

SEPTEMBER 1

Dear Jim,

I wanted to write you and let you know that I am still searching. It has not been as easy for me as it seems to be for others, but I am still trying.

I read the Bible every day and I am praying, although I am not certain to whom. I have read one of the books that you sent—about the missionary (China), and I have started *Basic Christianity*. Time is a problem.

I really appreciate the literature that you sent me and the time you spent talking with me on the phone. I am sorry that I know so little about Christians and all they believe.

The more I read and talk with others, the more I realize that my biggest obstacle is trust and faith. It is very difficult for me to depend on anyone or anything. I want to change.

When you told me that I needed to find Christ and then a church, I was astonished. Every day I remember those words, and I attempt prayer. It is awkward and seems childish to me—but I have continued.

I wanted to send you money for the books, but I didn't. Accepting gifts is another difficult thing for me. Someday I hope to repay you—hopefully by helping someone else as you have helped me.

I will keep trying and as soon as I can, I will write to you and say, "I know it's true. I know who He is." Thank you so much.

Until Then,
Vickie

SEPTEMBER 18

Dear Vickie,

Thank you for the very good, informative letter. In it, you said several things:

1. "I am still trying."
2. "My biggest obstacle is trust and faith."
3. "It is awkward and seems childish to me."
4. "Accepting gifts is a very difficult thing for me."
5. "I will keep trying."

Nos. 1 and 5: Quit trying. You cannot "trust" and "try" at the same time. "Trying" is your biggest problem. "Trying" says that it somehow depends on you. "Trusting" says that it depends on someone else. That would not be wise unless the someone else were trustworthy. Quit looking at and inspecting your faith. Instead, look at the faithfulness of God.

No. 2: Becoming a Christian does not take much faith, or strong faith. It takes very little faith in the very faithful God. In other words, God does the saving, not my faith. Trust and faith come from the Word of God. It is caused by the preaching of Christ—Romans 10:17. It is hindered by "trying" and by looking at your faith.

No. 3:

> Jesus said, "I tell you the truth, unless you change and become like little children, you will never enter the kingdom of Heaven. Therefore, whoever humbles himself like this child is the greatest in the kingdom of Heaven." (Matt.18:3–4)

> Jesus said, "Let the little children come to me, and do not hinder them, for the kingdom of God belongs to such as these. I tell you the truth, anyone who will not receive the kingdom of God like a little child will never enter it." (Luke 18:16–17)

In this case, childish is better. Children trust.

No. 4: The reason a gift is the only way is that Heaven is too expensive to buy. The only way it can be obtained is by the one who loves you and can afford to give it to you.

> For the wages of sin is death, but the gift of God is eternal life in Christ Jesus our Lord. (Rom. 6:23)

> At one time we too were foolish, disobedient, deceived and enslaved by all kinds of passions and pleasures. We lived in malice and envy, being hated and hating one another. But when the kindness and love of God our Savior appeared, he saved us, not because of righteous things we had done, but because of his mercy. He saved us through the washing of rebirth and

renewal by the Holy Spirit, whom he poured out on us generously through Jesus Christ our Savior, so that, having been justified by his grace, we might become heirs having the hope of eternal life. (Titus 3:3–7)

Please read John 1:1–4, Hebrews 1:1–4, and Colossians 1:13–20. These passages tell us two basic truths:

1. The Son of God, with the Father, is the Creator of everything and everyone. We belong to Him. He made us.
2. He redeemed us. That is, He bought us back by His death on the Cross. We belong to Him. He made us, and He bought us!

Please also read Romans 5:6–8 and Romans 4:24–25. I am not sure whether you have read the four Gospels: Matthew, Mark, Luke, and John. They are basic.

Remember, quit trying. Just respond to the truth as you read it. Do not fight the Scriptures.

In our Lord Jesus Christ,
Jim

SEPTEMBER 29

Dear Jim,

When I began to read your letter, I was so relieved. It made so much sense. I have been trying so hard . . . and getting nowhere; in fact, some things have gotten worse.

I have been waiting for some miracle—a bolt of lightning—anything, but nothing has happened. The Bible says that if I believe and ask, that is all that I can do. I have read, prayed, and asked. I will now turn the rest over to God. If it is to be, I'll let it be up to Him. This may be the biggest leap of faith in my whole life.

I really appreciate your letters and your call. I am so glad I wrote to you. It is people like you that make people like me want what you have. I have never met you, yet I know that you love the Lord with all of your heart. It shows in all that you have done for me. I will continue to read and pray. I will even pray for you! (It still sounds childish to me! I guess that's ok, too!) Tuesday I am going to start attending a Bible study on the book of John. I am excited!

You are a wonderful person—thank you.

Love Always,
Vickie

OCTOBER 9

Dear Vickie,

Thank you for your good letter. Let me quote you to you again. "I have been waiting for some miracle—a bolt of lightning—anything, but nothing has happened. The Bible says that if I believe and ask, that is all that I can do. I have read, prayed, and asked. I will now turn the rest over to God. If it is to be, I'll let it be up to Him. This may be the biggest leap of faith in my whole life."

As I mentioned in my last letter, you may be trying too hard. That may be the problem still. I would ask a question, but then I would have to wait for an answer, so instead I will guess and make a statement:

- When you read, you read with intensity.
- When you prayed, you prayed hard.
- When you asked, you asked with fervor.

You hoped that your intensity and fervor would bring down the bolt of lightning or anything. Even when you turned it over to God, you did it. Even when you made your big leap of faith, you really leaped (long and far).

Do you see that your reading, praying, asking, turning, leaping, and letting is still man-centered? Salvation is of God.

Now, brothers, I want to remind you of the gospel I preached to you, which you received and on which you have taken your stand. By this gospel you are saved, if you hold firmly to the work I preached to you. Otherwise, you have believed in vain. For what I received I passed on to you as of first importance: that Christ died for our sins according to the Scriptures, that he was buried, that he was raised on the third day according to the Scriptures, and that he appeared to Peter, and then to the Twelve. (1 Cor. 15:1–5)

It seems to me that you are putting more effort into "holding firmly" than you are to what you are holding.

It is the Word you are holding—His deity, death for our sins, His burial, and resurrection.

Please focus on 1) the holiness of God, 2) your sinfulness in the light of His holiness, and 3) His grace toward you, which is much greater than your sinfulness (Rom. 5:20).

Please do not put your faith in your faith.

Assuming you have evaluated your trying, here is my suggestion if you can say this to God without working up a fervent prayer. "God, have mercy on me, a sinner" (Luke 18:13) and "Thank you for my salvation and forgiveness of sins in Jesus' name."

You will see the following evidence in your life: love for the Christians (1 John 3:14, John 13:34–35), obedience (1 John 2:3), understanding (1 Corinthians 2:14), the fruit of the Spirit (Galatians 5:19–23), taking Him at His word (John 5:24), chastening (Hebrews 12:5–11).

This is only true for real Christians. If you do not see this in your life, then you are still on the outside. However, I think this will not be the case.

> In our Lord Jesus Christ,
> Jim

OCTOBER 12

Dear Vickie,

This afternoon I was reading Mark 10. I would like you to read and compare the stories of the rich young ruler, starting with Mark 10:17, and blind Bartimaeus, starting with verse 46. After you read the stories, look at this:

The Rich Young Man	Blind Bartimaeus
1.	rich	begging
2.	running	sitting
3.	healthy	blind—threw away his coat
4.	"What must I do to inherit eternal life?"	"Son of David, have mercy on me."
5.	6 commands (Jesus)	"What do you want me to do for you?"
6.	"I've done them." (rich man)	"Rabbi, I want to see." (Bartimaeus)
7.	"You lack one thing. Sell, give, and follow me." (Jesus)	"Go, your faith has healed you."
8.	He went away sad.	Immediately he received his sight and followed Jesus.

The first man thought he could do it and couldn't and went away sad. The second man knew he couldn't and so trusted Jesus 100%.

Dear Vickie, I trust you have become like Bartimaeus, for that is the way.

In our Lord Jesus Christ,
Jim

OCTOBER 19

Dear Jim,

Thanks so much for your last letter. It makes so much sense; it is meant to be easy, simple, and free.

You guessed correctly on everything I have been trying to do. I have taken your suggestions. I prayed as you wrote. Every day I ask God to come into my life and lead me in whatever direction he chooses. I still take control much of the time, but more and more I am asking God for help.

I don't understand many things. The whys are many. It is hard for me to comprehend the kind of love that God offers. I have spent so much time thinking about it—I decided to just stop. It has always been hard for me to comprehend anyone really loving me. I'm sure this is a childhood thing—but it has followed me into adulthood. God loves me, and with his help, I will learn to accept that.

I read the two stories in Mark about the rich man and the blind man. I don't consider myself rich—but when compared with others, I have been fortunate. I want a relationship with God. My survival instincts have literally kept me alive through difficult times. Lately I have realized what my survival instincts are and have always been—God. People have always admired my ability to endure things that they think they couldn't have. Even though I never asked, I realize now I never did endure them alone. God has taken care of me. I can look back and see it so clearly now. The pain I've seen in my life should have ended my life—but it didn't. I have always felt there had to be a reason to go on, putting one foot in front of the other—hoping for a brighter tomorrow—knowing always that other people had dealt with worse circumstances than I. Trying to smile no matter what was hard, but I always did—because God was taking care.

Every day I will thank God for loving me—enough to watch his son endure terrible pain on my behalf. I can't imagine how much it would hurt to watch—knowing you could stop it if you wanted to. I need to invite God into my life 100 times a day because I keep trying too hard. With his help I will learn, and he can change me.

I love your letters—someday we will meet. Thank you so much for caring enough to take the time to write and call.

I feel so overwhelmed at times—it is so amazing! I am astonished at how clear it seems. I can hardly think about anything else.

Jim, I know you walk with God. I will pray for you—and your work. I hope you realize how much you have been an instrument in helping me. I am sure you have helped many, with God's help. Someday, if God chooses, I will help someone, too.

My Love Always,
Vickie

OCTOBER 24

Dear Vickie,

Your letter of the nineteenth arrived today. This answer will be short. First I will quote you to yourself:

"Every day I ask God to come into my life and lead me in whatever direction he chooses." "I need to invite God into my life 100 times a day because I keep trying too hard."

You ask God every day and think you should ask 100 times a day.

No, you should not ask God 100 times a day, nor even once every day. The only reason for that would be if He came in and then left. You do not need to ask more than once in a lifetime if in fact He responded to your request. (Actually, you do not need to ask at all—see "Christmas is coming . . . " below.) If He did come in, He said, "I will never leave you nor forsake you" (Heb. 13:5); and "I give them eternal life, and they shall never perish; no one can snatch them out of my hand. My father, who has given them to me, is greater than all; no one can snatch them out of my Father's hand. I and the Father are one"(John 10:28–30); and the last half of Romans 8, actually verses 31–39.

Quit asking! Thank Him! You may do that 100 times a day.

Again, to quote you, "It makes so much sense; it is meant to be easy, simple and free."

Christmas is coming. Friends and relatives will have gifts for you. They are already paid for, wrapped with your name on them. Will you go to each of these givers and "ask" for your gift? Will you have to ask 100 times? You will not have to ask at all. You can walk away, not receive, not unwrap, and leave them there. You can reject them, but you do not need to ask for them. Your salvation is bought and paid for, and with your name on it.

> Therefore, if anyone is in Christ, he is a new creation; the old has gone, the new has come! All this is from God, who reconciled us to Himself through Christ, not counting men's sins against them. And He has committed to us the message of reconciliation. We are therefore Christ's ambassadors, as though God were making His appeal through us. We implore you on Christ's behalf: Be reconciled to God. God made Him who had no sin to be sin for us, so that in Him we might become the righteousness of God. (2 Cor 5:17–21)

I am asking you on behalf of Christ, "be reconciled to God." You do not ask; He is doing the asking. You receive and thank Him.

You have not told me any of your life. This is not a request to hear it. You have told me enough to let me know that you are a "survivor," a non-quitter. This is why it has been hard to trust God. He might not be trustworthy, so you have trusted yourself.

However, now you know better.

Forget the "whys." If they were given to you, would it be for you to determine whether the answers were adequate? If the room is dark, you do not ask "how" or "why" electricity works before you turn on the light.

You did not refuse to be born because you did not know "how" or "why" your brain, heart, and kidneys

worked. You did not insist on a PhD in physiology before you were born.

The "whys" will be answered later, or perhaps they
will not matter to you.

In our Lord Jesus Christ,

Jim

NOVEMBER 1

Dear Jim,

I have been so fortunate to have you be a part of my
life. Your letters have come to mean so much to me.
It is almost [as] if you can sense what I am thinking.
Thank you so much for taking time for me. Thank you
so much for your patience.

When I read your letters, I am almost embarrassed
of my lack of knowledge. You have been so right with
your insights.

I am reading in Revelation this week, or I will be
reading in Revelation beginning tomorrow morning. I
know that I will need to read, study, and pray for years
to have the understanding of the scriptures that you
do. Hopefully God will give me that opportunity.

I have asked for God's guidance on choosing a
church to attend. I am still waiting for an answer. I
don't feel like I know enough to make that decision. I
do want to be baptized though. I told Brad that I would
love it if you were able to baptize me. I am not sure
what the "traditions" are with baptism. Do you have to

be baptized by a "church leader?" My experience with religions certainly won't answer that question for me.

I feel like I need to write a letter to the Catholic Church and let them know what I believe to be true now. I'm sure my leaving will seem insignificant to them. My Godparents probably will be upset.

It is funny how I have been hearing from people that I haven't heard from in years, since I have come to know Jesus. I can't wait to share it with them!

I know I haven't shared much of my life with you. I am thirty-five, married, with two children. This is the second marriage for my husband and myself. My husband had two children from his previous marriage— but they died (a rare disease). We buried his youngest two years ago, his oldest five years ago. It has been quite tragic and painful for the entire family, especially my husband. He is very bitter. He says he doesn't believe in God, that he is agnostic. But in the same breath he will tell you he would hate a God that could allow his daughters to suffer so long and so hard. I have been praying for him every day.

I have raised two agnostic children—one in college—one in middle school. They are not much different from their mother. But they do love and respect me. They are great kids, but they don't know the Lord. I am praying for them every day, too.

My background was a mixture of abuse and abuses. My mother was (and still is) an alcoholic. When I was old enough to "control," I ran away. I gave birth to my son when I was sixteen. My life, because of my own bad choices (drugs, alcohol, men) deteriorated from there. When I was twenty-one (a very "old lady" by this time), I stopped using drugs. I became pregnant again, married (just not the father of my child). We moved to California. He wasn't faithful. We moved back to Utah and divorced shortly afterwards. I did develop a relationship again with my daughter's father (my son's father was dead) on a friendship basis only. He developed a relationship with our daughter, though. He became part of "our family" (my current husband, too). He (my daughter's father) passed away two years ago shortly after my stepdaughter.

With all of the illness, pain, struggle, and death in my life over the past few years, I have realized how fortunate I have been. I have immediate family members who have not been as fortunate.

I have been successful in business. I love my husband and my children. All of the material things I lacked as a child, my children have enjoyed. I have educated myself, educated my children, indulged in all of the joys that money can buy—AND I HAVE FELT AS EMPTY AS I DID AS A CHILD.

I am smiling for the first time in my life because I actually feel joy. (Before, the smile and jokes had been a mask.) There is no doubt in my mind that God has helped me survive even though I didn't know him. Now that I know him and am learning more about him every day, I can hardly describe how happy I am. He is starting to work in my life. This is the first time I have ever felt loved for nothing I have done. The love in my life previously has been conditional, or at least I've felt that way.

I never knew my biological father, although I can remember one visit with him. I loved him without ever knowing him. I started a search for him about six months ago and found out he was dead. He died only four years ago. If I had begun my search earlier, I could have known him. I never had a father figure in my life. I never will. If I had never written to you, I might not have started my search for God. Now that I have found him, I don't want to lose him! Thank you again for helping me.

Love,
Your sister—in Christ! Vickie

DECEMBER 11

Dear Jim,

I haven't written for so long—and I do miss your return letters. I hope that all is well with you and your family.

I have been very busy with work, too busy. I have felt so depressed for the last two weeks. I have been sitting here trying to figure out why, and I think I have. I haven't been reading and studying every day like I was. I haven't been praying as often as I was either. Last night I read and prayed, and I felt better. Today I haven't yet and the depression is creeping in again. And so I decided to write a letter to you (that I've meant to write for some time now), and then settle down to read.

This time of year has always been difficult for me to enjoy. I was hoping that this year would be different, but I can see that I will have to make it different. I need to focus on Jesus and make him the center of my life. I know if I will do that, everything else will be ok. I don't know why I don't just do it, why I make it so hard!

One of these days I am going to drive up there and meet you. If by chance you do get down this way before I get there, please let me know.

A question for you: Last night we were reading John chapter 11. When someone dies, do they go immediately to heaven? If so, then what is the resurrection? If not, where are they until the resurrection? Is there more than one resurrection? When Jesus was raised from the dead, he had a physical body—will we? I was just wondering.

Have a great Christmas, and an even greater New Year!

Love,

Vickie

DECEMBER 16

Dear Vickie,

Your letter arrived this morning with your gift for the family. Thank you very much!

Your evaluation is right (or partly right). Time with God in the Bible and in prayer is a major means of staying in the joy of the Lord. The other part is not preventative; it is curative. It is called confession of sin. I will send to you today a cassette tape on the subject with a piece of paper that will help the talk make sense to you. In the meantime, please read 1 John 1:5–10. Read it several times. After reading the paragraph, notice the positive good truth in the odd-numbered verses and the negative bad truth in the even-numbered verses. Practice verses 7 and 9 based upon verse 5. Do not practice verses 6, 8, and 10. Read the rest of 1 John, noticing and marking the word "know."

Now to your questions concerning the resurrection of the body.

We go immediately to Heaven when we die, without our body. We leave that here.

For to me, to live is Christ and to die is gain. If I am to go on living in the body, this will mean fruitful labor for me. Yet what shall I choose? I do not know! I am torn between the two: I desire to depart and be with Christ, which is better by far; but it is more necessary for you that I remain in the body. (Phil. 1:21–24)

See also 2 Corinthians 5:6–9.

The resurrection occurs when Jesus Christ returns to earth.

Brothers, we do not want you to be ignorant about those who fall asleep, or to grieve like the rest of men, who have no hope. We believe that Jesus died and rose again and so we believe that God will bring with Jesus those who have fallen asleep in him. According to the Lord's own word, we tell you that we who are still alive, who are left till the coming of the Lord, will certainly not precede those who have fallen asleep. For the Lord himself will come down from heaven, with a loud command, with the voice of the archangel and with the trumpet call of God, and the dead in Christ will rise first. After that, we who are still alive and are left will be caught up together with them in the clouds to meet the Lord in the air. And so we will be with the Lord forever. Therefore encourage each other with these words. (1 Thess. 4:13–18)

1 Corinthians 15:47–54 is another Scripture on this event.

We will have a physical body just like Jesus, but only after He returns.

But our citizenship is in heaven. And we eagerly await a Savior from there, the Lord Jesus Christ, who, by the power that enables him to bring everything under his control, will transform our lowly bodies so that they will be like his glorious body. (Phil. 3:20–21)

Also see 1 John 3:1–3, Titus 2:11–14, and Romans 8:22–25.

Yours in our Lord Jesus Christ,
Jim

The Gospel

Jim Wilson

If you confess with your mouth, "Jesus is Lord," and believe in your heart that God raised him from the dead, you will be saved. (Rom. 10:9)

---

*H*aving read this booklet, you may realize that you are not a Christian. If you are a Christian, you can be delivered from the awful sin of bitterness. If you are not a Christian, your bitterness is tied up with many other sins and with a nature that is prone to sin. In order to get rid of the bitterness, you need a new nature, and you need to get rid of your old nature. You cannot do this yourself. It can be done only by God.

Here is your part:

1. You need to want to be set free from the guilt and judgement for your sins and from the power of sin.

2. You need to know that you are helpless in this want.

3. You need to know that being good and not being bad will not set you free, nor will any other means of self-effort.

4. You need to know that God has already accomplished this deliverance by sending the Lord Jesus to earth to die for the ungodly. "You see, at just the right time, when we were still powerless, Christ died for the ungodly" (Rom. 5:6).

5. Three days after this death for our sins, the Lord Jesus rose from the dead in order to make us righteous. "He was delivered over to death for our sins and was raised to life for our justification" (Rom. 4:25).

6. The Holy Spirit is now drawing you to turn from your sin, to call upon the Lord Jesus, trusting Him, His death, and His resurrection.

That if you confess with your mouth, "Jesus is Lord," and believe in your heart that God raised him from the dead, you will be saved. For it is with your heart that you believe and are justified, and it is with your mouth that you confess and are saved. (Rom. 10:9–10)

Now, brothers, I want to remind you of the gospel I preached to you, which you received and on which you have taken your stand. By this gospel you are saved, if you hold firmly to the word I preached to you. Otherwise, you have believed in vain. For what I received I passed on to you as of first importance: that Christ died for our sins according to the Scriptures, that he was buried, that he was raised on the third day according to the Scriptures, and that he appeared to Peter, and then to the Twelve. (1 Cor. 15:1–5)

Now that you have called upon the Lord Jesus, thank Him for bringing you to the Father, for forgiving your sin, and for giving you everlasting life.

Now, in your joy of your forgiveness, tell someone what God has done for you.

If you write to us, we will send you books to help you grow in the Christian life.

Reader Letters

Greetings to you, dear Uncle Jim,

I praise God for bringing me in fellowship with you.

I have been privileged to read your message "being free from bitterness." I really needed this part in my life as I have been in this sin often without recognition. Recently, I was struggling with bitterness towards a person and could not love as I ought to as a Christian. Was given your message on bitterness to be read by my husband. I prayerfully read your message and was convicted of my sin. As you said, I neither kept it struggling in my heart nor went to the person and shared about it, but went right to God on my knees and confessed my sin. God helped me to come out of that bitterness towards that person and is helping me to love her.

I really thank you very much for that wonderful, life-changing message in order to become like our Savior...

I am Chaitanya David, wife of C Stephen David from India (Discipleship Training Centre). I need your prayers so that God would reveal more and more of my sins and help me to deal and deny myself and enable me to carry my cross following Jesus Christ.

Your message out of God's Word is a blessing in my life and I pray it would be in many others' lives.

Your daughter in Christ,
Chaitanya David
Hyderabad, India

Greetings,

Thanks for the word. Just thought I would say thanks again for the book on bitterness. Yesterday I was visiting an inmate who thanked me again for the book. He is in for domestic violence and over the last few months I have seen his very hard appearance melt away . . .

Thanks,
Rich

Dear Sirs,

My name is ———. I am currently a prisoner in Multnomah County Jail, serving a 180-day [sentence] for public drunkenness and disorderly conduct.

Recently I retrieved your pamphlet from the trash and after drying it out, found it to be the most powerful and timely gift to help my broken mind, body, and spirit.

It never leaves my side and is now ragged. Many many people want one, but I only let them copy parts by hand to show their truthful wants.

No one in the chaplain's office knows where your booklet came from, as they say they've never seen one or had one before. You and I know exactly where it came from. It has changed my life and behavior . . .

May God bless you for bringing light and hope back into my life through His Word.

God bless you and keep you!

Dear Jim,

I read the booklet "How To Get Rid of Bitterness" in late 1993. It was a sort of revelation from the Lord that made me feel I should begin my life anew but first I was to forgive my husband (we were divorced for 10 years already and there was no day and no place for me to curse him again and again) and there was also my friend, my colleague (we had been bosom friends for 14 years before she betrayed me when I got a chance to get a very high position and to move to the capital to the Presidium of the Academy of Sciences). I read and reread the booklet and could not overcome my profound astonishment at how stupid it was of me to feel that bitterness because of them, for me who knew Jesus so well and found all the drawbacks of my life on learning what He teaches. I began to pray for the Lord to set me free from this sin. There were no cleansing tears I used to have when I repented and received Christ as my Savior, but I felt such bliss and rejoicing that I prayed and prayed and I felt I am becoming a different person. It was long ago and now I remember that there were such people in my life but this memory is not in my heart this memory is sort of a dry fact as $2 \times 2 = 4$. I was happy and I HAVE BEEN happy to have this God's weapon against bitterness.

All my friends have a Russian copy of the booklet and from all of them I heard, "Nell, how simple and how great. I am so happy to be taught this truth that liberates." I do not know who gave me that book because there was a very big team from America, and they brought many good books. But my understanding is that it was God's angel who put it among other books or else I could devastate myself with the bitterness I felt. And you can hardly imagine how happy I was to receive a personal letter from JIM WILSON himself. God's will be done.

Nellie Provolotskaya
Novosibirsk, Russia

Jim,

. . . I am 38 years old and have been a Christian my whole life . . . Since I was in my early teens I have had dry and cracked skin on my fingers that would bleed and peel and was quite painful. In 25 years I have tried every known treatment for dry skin from the medical field, from family remedies, and things that were given to me by friends and family that were concerned about my condition. I was even treated by the U.S. Air Force's head of dermatology when I was in basic training in Texas. I have never had more than mild improvement and even treatments that helped were not effective for long. I tried moisturizers and rubber or cotton gloves when I slept and even used them at work on some of the worst days.

When I received your Bitterness book I packed it in my bag and deployed the next day to Saudi Arabia as part of Air Expeditionary Force #6. I read the book on the way over and again when I got there. After thinking about it for a while I finally realized that maybe it was the bitterness that I held towards many people that was my problem; I believed that the dry skin was the manifestation of my bitterness. I offered the bitterness (and the dry skin) up and have strived since then to clear up past wrongs where I could, and to let go of hurt and anger in all instances. I am happy to say that by the time I got home 45 days later I had normal skin again for the first time in 25 years, and it is still fine four months later. I review the Bitterness book weekly and strive to keep myself bitterness-free and living in the Word.

Have a great day and thanks again. God's Blessings to you and your Ministry.

Tony

Dear Jim,

Greetings today and just a short note—another testimony about your little booklet on bitterness and forgiveness. That booklet came unexpectedly in the mail a few days before I went on some active duty time to Quantico. I threw it into my briefcase as I packed, thinking that I would read it on the trip. Later I did, noting how helpful it was.

After a class day in Quantico an officer came up to me and asked for my advice. This reserve Major was a lawyer working in the Pentagon. She wanted to know if she should bring legal charges against the Col. she worked for. The next day she handed me a legally prepared document 20 pages long chronicling the offenses she was keeping against this man for the last six months. None seemed really serious to me but they were obviously taking an enormous toll on her health. I asked that before we talk she read something that I would give her. So she read your booklet on how to be free from bitterness. It struck right to the point for her and although she had been brought up in the church, it confronted her in a very meaningful way. Later, in dealing with the matter of her boss (and some other serious hurts from the past) I had the opportunity to share the Gospel in a life-changing way for her. In the process of that discussion I asked her if she would die that day, did she know what would happen to her, etc. Here is what was so significant to me. She said, "After reading that book on bitterness, I don't know what would happen to me." It was evident to me that your message for her was the preaching of the law, and it was showing her a need and driving her to Christ. I rejoiced to see how God used that message and continue to pray for her that God would establish her in the faith . . .

Still appreciating your friendship and leadership in Christ Jesus,

Sincerely,

Steve

Dear Jim,

I don't think that we have met face to face, but I enjoy reading your emails and have heard about you for years. I am a '74 USNA grad. I read your Bitterness book several years ago and would like to give you a brief testimony. I have been in Christian ministry for about 22 years on staff with the Navigators. I was trapped by the lies that my significance was based on 'rank' or 'title' and when I did not receive 'promotions' I became bitter. This bitterness lingered and once set in, became the 'root' for many other perceived offenses to take hold of me leading to more episodes where I felt I had the 'right' to be bitter. The pathetic thing is that everyone around me could see it, but I couldn't. It was right out of Psa. 73, "When my soul was embittered, when I was pricked in heart, I was stupid and ignorant...." After reading your booklet, for the first time I saw that bitterness is and by itself a 'sin'. I asked God to show me every root of bitterness that was in me. In a short period of time, I was able to list 16 different roots of bitterness. I took time to confess each one, one by one and asking God for forgiveness. Then I called my supervisor and confessed all 16 to him and asked him for forgiveness. God graciously forgave me and set me free. I have to guard my soul, for it has proven to be a fertile ground for bitter seeds to dwell. I must diligently guard my thoughts to prevent any of the previous 16 items from taking root again.

Thanks for your booklet and teaching. It is much needed in the body of Christ.

In Christ,

Bob

Afterword

You have probably found out from reading this booklet that you are bitter or offended or a gossip or depressed or have a poor relationship with your parents. If you do not understand the solutions given in the booklet, if you do understand but find yourself unable to put them into effect, or if you do not want to change, it is possible that there is a more basic problem, that is, you are not a Christian. Please reread Letters on Becoming a Christian and The Gospel. Please contact us. We can send you a free New Testament and other literature that will be helpful for your particular needs. That way we can communicate clearly the simple and profound truths of the good news of Jesus Christ in a personal way.

Community Christian Ministries
Attn: Jim Wilson
P.O. Box 9754
Moscow, ID 83843
Phone: (208) 883–0997
E-mail: ccm@moscow.com
Online: ccmbooks.org

You can contact any of the authors of this volume through the same address.

9 f this book has been a help to you, please help spread the word to others by leaving a review on Amazon, Goodreads, or your favorite site.

To find out more about Community Christian Ministries, join our mailing list at ccmbooks.org or scan the QR code below. We give away more copies of this book than we sell; if you are interested in supporting this or any of CCM's other ministries, you can donate on our website or by check to the address above.

Made in United States
North Haven, CT
06 August 2022

22323612R10095